Harvard
Business
Review

ON
ORGANIZATIONAL
LEARNING

THE HARVARD BUSINESS REVIEW PAPERBACK SERIES

The series is designed to bring today's managers and professionals the fundamental information they need to stay competitive in a fast-moving world. From the preeminent thinkers whose work has defined an entire field to the rising stars who will redefine the way we think about business, here are the leading minds and landmark ideas that have established the *Harvard Business Review* as required reading for ambitious businesspeople in organizations around the globe.

Other books in the series:

Other books in the series (continued):

Harvard Business Review

ON

ORGANIZATIONAL LEARNING

A HARVARD BUSINESS REVIEW PAPERBACK

The *Harvard Business Review* articles in this collection are available as
individual reprints. Discounts apply to quantity purchases. For information and ordering, please contact Customer Service, Harvard Business
School Publishing, Boston, MA 02163. Telephone: (617) 783-7500 or
(800) 988-0886, 8 A.M. to 6 P.M. Eastern Time, Monday through Friday.
Fax: (617) 783-7555, 24 hours a day. E-mail: custserv@hbsp.harvard.edu

978-1-57851-615-5 (ISBN 13)
Library of Congress Cataloging-in-Publication Data
Harvard business review on organizational learning.
        p.   cm. — (Harvard business review paperback series)
    Includes index.
    ISBN 1-57851-615-3
    1. Organizational learning. 2. Knowledge management.
I. Harvard business review.   II. Series.
HD58.82 .H37 2001
658.4´038—dc21   2001016925
                                                                              CIP

Contents

Harvard Business Review

ON

ORGANIZATIONAL
LEARNING

Communities of Practice

The Organizational Frontier

ETIENNE C. WENGER AND
WILLIAM M. SNYDER

Executive Summary

A NEW ORGANIZATIONAL FORM is emerging in companies that run on knowledge: the community of practice. And for this expanding universe of companies, communities of practice promise to radically galvanize
knowledge sharing, learning, and change.

A community of practice is a group of people informally bound together by shared expertise and passion
for a joint enterprise. People in companies form them for
a variety of reasons—to maintain connections with peers
when the company reorganizes; to respond to external
changes such as the rise of e-commerce; to meet new
challenges when the company changes strategy.

Regardless of the circumstances that give rise to communities of practice, their members inevitably share
knowledge in free-flowing, creative ways that foster new
approaches to problems. Over the past five years, the

authors have seen communities of practice improve performance at companies as diverse as an international bank, a major car manufacturer, and a U.S. government agency. Communities of practice can drive strategy, generate new lines of business, solve problems, promote the spread of best practices, develop people's skills, and help companies recruit and retain talent.

The paradox of such communities is that although they are self-organizing and thus resistant to supervision and interference, they do require specific managerial efforts to develop them and integrate them into an organization. Only then can they be fully leveraged.

The authors explain the steps managers need to take in order to get communities going—and to sustain them so they can become a central part of their companies' success.

TODAY'S ECONOMY RUNS on knowledge, and most companies work assiduously to capitalize on that fact. They use cross-functional teams, customer- or product-focused business units, and work groups—to name just a few organizational forms—to capture and spread ideas and know-how. In many cases, these ways of organizing are very effective, and no one would argue for their demise. But a new organizational form is emerging that promises to complement existing structures and radically galvanize knowledge sharing, learning, and change. It's called the community of practice.

What are communities of practice? In brief, they're groups of people informally bound together by shared expertise and passion for a joint enterprise—engineers engaged in deep-water drilling, for example, consultants

who specialize in strategic marketing, or frontline
managers in charge of check processing at a large commercial bank. Some communities of practice meet
regularly—for lunch on Thursdays, say. Others are connected primarily by e-mail networks. A community of
practice may or may not have an explicit agenda on a
given week, and even if it does, it may not follow the
agenda closely. Inevitably, however, people in communities of practice share their experiences and knowledge in
free-flowing, creative ways that foster new approaches to
problems.

Because its primary "output"—knowledge—is intangible, the community of practice might sound like
another "soft" management fad. But that's not the case.
During the past five years, we have seen communities of
practice improve organizational performance at companies as diverse as an international bank, a major car
manufacturer, and a U.S. government agency. Communities of practice can drive strategy, generate new lines of
business, solve problems, promote the spread of best
practices, develop people's professional skills, and help
companies recruit and retain talent. (For examples of
how communities of practice have helped companies,
see "Communities in Action" at the end of this article.)

If communities of practice are so effective, why aren't
they more prevalent? There are three reasons. The first is
that although communities of practice have been around
for a long time—for centuries, in fact—the term has just
recently entered the business vernacular. The second is
that only several dozen forward-thinking companies
have taken the leap of "installing" or nurturing them.
The third reason is that it's not particularly easy to build
and sustain communities of practice or to integrate
them with the rest of an organization. The organic,

spontaneous, and informal nature of communities of practice makes them resistant to supervision and interference.

But we have observed a number of companies that have overcome the managerial paradox inherent in communities of practice and successfully nurtured them. In general, we have found that managers cannot mandate communities of practice. Instead, successful managers bring the right people together, provide an infrastructure in which communities can thrive, and measure the communities' value in nontraditional ways. These tasks of cultivation aren't easy, but the harvest they yield makes them well worth the effort.

The Hallmarks of Communities of Practice

Communities of practice were common as far back as ancient times. In classical Greece, for instance, "corporations" of metalworkers, potters, masons, and other craftsmen had both a social purpose (members worshiped the same deities and celebrated holidays together) and a business function (members trained apprentices and spread innovations). In the Middle Ages, guilds played similar roles for artisans throughout Europe. Today's communities of practice are different in one important respect: instead of being composed primarily of people working on their own, they often exist within large organizations.

Communities of practice are as diverse as the situations that give rise to them. People in companies form them for a variety of reasons. For example, when a company reorganizes into a team-based structure, employees with functional expertise may create communities of practice as a way of maintaining connections with peers. Elsewhere, people may form communities in response to changes originating outside the organization, such as the rise of e-commerce, or inside, such as new company strategies—think of auto manufacturers going into the financing business or computer makers offering consulting services.

A community of practice can exist entirely within a business unit or stretch across divisional boundaries. A community can even thrive with members from different companies; for example, the CEOs who make up the Business Roundtable meet regularly to discuss relationships between business and public policy, among other things. A community can be made up of tens or even hundreds of people, but typically it has a core of participants whose passion for the topic energizes the community and who provide intellectual and social leadership. Large communities are often subdivided by geographic region or by subject matter in order to encourage people to take part actively.

Communities of practice differ from other forms of organization in several ways. (For a summary of the differences, see the exhibit "A Snapshot Comparison.") Consider, briefly, how communities differ from teams. Teams are created by managers to complete specific projects. Managers select team members on the basis of their ability to contribute to the team's goals, and the group disbands once the project has been finished. Communities of practice, on the other hand, are informal— they organize themselves, meaning they set their own agendas and establish their own leadership. And membership in a community of practice is self-selected. In other words, people in such communities tend to know when and if they should join. They know if they have something to give and whether they are likely to take something away. And members of an existing community, when they invite someone to join, also operate on a gut sense of the prospective member's appropriateness for the group.

To get a better sense of how communities of practice look in action, let's consider two examples.

At the Hill's Pet Nutrition facility in Richmond, Indiana, line technicians meet weekly to talk about recent successes and frustrations as well as challenges looming ahead. They formed the group several years ago after managers and technicians attended a retreat where they were introduced to the concept of communities of practice and learned how such groups could help the company develop and retain technical expertise. The group has a "mayor" who's been chosen by his peers to keep things on track from week to week and see to it that people with relevant expertise are present when needed. The plant grants people time to participate. Actual attendance fluctuates depending on the agenda.

At a recent gathering we observed, 12 technicians from the first and second shifts met around a large table in the glass-walled conference room overlooking the plant. Although it was midafternoon, they were soon joined by Roger, a technician from the third shift who would have to return seven hours later to begin his "real" work. Roger made a special trip in on this occasion to help John hone his proposal to substitute pneumatic tubes for the balky conveyor belt that carried the pet food kibbles to the packaging bin; Roger's background in plumbing was thus particularly relevant.

Senior managers at the plant had not warmed to the pneumatic tube idea. They believed the conveyor system would work if people just operated it properly. They felt the new approach was unproven and, in any case, would be difficult to incorporate with the plant's current technology. Nevertheless, community members had encour-

A Snapshot Comparison

Communities of practice, formal work groups, teams, and informal networks are useful in complementary ways. Below is a summary of their characteristics.

	What's the purpose?	Who belongs?	What holds it together?	How long does it last?
Community of practice	To develop members' capabilities; to build and exchange knowledge	Members who select themselves	Passion, commitment, and identification with the group's expertise	As long as there is interest in maintaining the group
Formal work group	To deliver a product or service	Everyone who reports to the group's manager	Job requirements and common goals	Until the next reorganization
Project team	To accomplish a specified task	Employees assigned by senior management	The project's milestones and goals	Until the project has been completed
Informal network	To collect and pass on business information	Friends and business acquaintances	Mutual needs	As long as people have a reason to connect

aged John to continue pushing for change, and John had pressed on, buoyed by the knowledge that experts in his community of practice saw merit in his proposal.

Before the group members took up John's proposal, they followed their usual opening routine—going around the table and letting people vent about one thing or another, including the most recent Colts game. They also followed up on the previous week's discussion about rethinking how new technicians are certified. Then they turned to the proposal.

Vince began by reviewing management's concerns. John then explained that the latest revision of his proposal included evidence from colleagues in other plants that the technology was reliable and would be compatible with existing equipment. Roger was able to confirm the evidence based on his own experience and suggested that he go along the next time John presented his ideas to management.

The community support for John's work ultimately paid off. A year after the meeting, the company installed the new technology. The result? Significant reductions in downtime and wasted pet food related to packaging. In addition to benefiting the company in this way, the community provides important benefits for members: it gives them opportunities to solve nagging problems and hone their ability to run the plant effectively. Improvements in operations can lead to financial rewards in the form of bonuses that are tied to the plant's performance.

Our second example comes from Hewlett-Packard, where a community of practice consisting of product-delivery consultants from around North America holds monthly teleconferences. The community focuses on an HP software product called High Availability, which minimizes computer downtime for customers. The core group of consultants, who had been somewhat isolated, came together a few years ago with the help of facilitators from a knowledge management support team. The members discovered that they had many problems in common and that they could learn a great deal from one another. The community has succeeded in standardizing the software's sales and installation processes and establishing a consistent pricing scheme for HP salespeople.

Participation in the monthly calls is voluntary, but levels of attendance are steady. For one such call, the focus was meant to be on Maureen's experiences with a major customer for which she was installing the product. Before diving in, however, the consultants spent the first ten minutes chatting about the recent reorganization of their division—whether it was a good thing, what it meant for them, and so on.

Maureen hadn't spent a lot of time preparing a formal presentation; she knew that only by talking directly and openly could she spur the give-and-take that would make the call worthwhile for the group. As the call proceeded, community members interrupted her constantly with questions and examples from their own experiences—all of which helped Maureen understand how to work more effectively with her clients.

The conversation then turned to a persistent bug in the software. Rob, a member of the software division that developed the product, had been invited to take part in these calls to create a stronger connection between the product-delivery consultants and software developers. He'd already worked out a way to get rid of the bug, but he learned from the stories he heard in the tele-

As communities of practice generate knowledge, they renew themselves. They give you both the golden eggs and the goose that lays them.

conference how to make the fix even more effective. He told the group that he would follow up during next month's call.

The participants in these communities of practice were learning together by focusing on problems that were directly related to their work. In the short term, this made their work easier or more effective; in the long term, it helped build both their communities and their shared practices—thus developing capabilities critical to the continuing success of the organizations.

The strength of communities of practice is self-perpetuating. As they generate knowledge, they reinforce and renew themselves. That's why communities of practice give you not only the golden eggs but also the goose that lays them. The farmer killed the goose to get all the gold and ended up losing both; the challenge for organizations is to appreciate the goose and to understand how to keep it alive and productive.

A Paradox of Management

Although communities of practice are fundamentally informal and self-organizing, they benefit from cultivation. Like gardens, they respond to attention that respects their nature. You can't tug on a cornstalk to make it grow faster or taller, and you shouldn't yank a marigold out of the ground to see if it has roots. You can, however, till the soil, pull out weeds, add water during dry spells, and ensure that your plants have the proper nutrients. And while you may welcome the wildflowers that bloom without any cultivation, you may get even more satisfaction from those vegetables and flowers you started from seed.

The same is true for companies that grow communi-

ties of practice from seed. To get communities going—
and to sustain them over time—managers should:

- identify potential communities of practice that will
  enhance the company's strategic capabilities;

- provide the infrastructure that will support such communities and enable them to apply their expertise
  effectively;

- use nontraditional methods to assess the value of the
  company's communities of practice.

IDENTIFYING POTENTIAL COMMUNITIES

Communities of practice should not be created in a vac-
uum. In most cases, informal networks of people with
the ability and the passion to further develop an organization's core competencies already exist. The task is to
identify such groups and help them come together as
communities of practice. At Shell, for example, a person
who wants to develop a new community joins forces
with a consultant and interviews prospective members.
They look at challenges and problems that people across
units and teams have in common and that would serve
as bases for a community of practice. The interviews are
not only a means of collecting information; they also
generate enthusiasm for the embryonic community.
After laying the groundwork, the coordinator calls the
members of the community of practice together, and the
group begins discussing plans for activities that will
build individual and group capabilities and advance the
company's strategic agenda.

A key task is defining a community's domain. If members don't feel personally connected to the group's area
of expertise and interest once it has been defined, they

won't fully commit themselves to the work of the community. The U.S. Veterans Administration found this to be true with a community it started in its claims-processing organization. The core group first defined its focus as "technical capability," an umbrella term coveing employees' processing skills and the associated procedures and equipment. During the community's first year, the core group's participation was limited and progress was slow. The more active members decided they could move faster if they redefined the community's domain. They created subcommunities of first-line managers, customer service representatives, and training coordinators. As a result, the first-line managers are sharing tips about implementing a new team structure, the customer service reps are helping to set standards to reduce processing time, and the training coordinators are upgrading training modules across the organization.

Executives must invest time and money in helping communities reach their full potential. That means intervening when they run up against obstacles.

PROVIDING THE INFRASTRUCTURE

Communities of practice are vulnerable because they lack the legitimacy—and the budgets—of established departments. To reach their full potential, then, they need to be integrated into the business and supported in specific ways.

Senior executives must be prepared to invest time and money in helping such communities reach their full potential. That means intervening when communities run up against obstacles to their progress, such as IT systems that don't serve them, promotion systems that overlook community contributions, and reward structures that discourage collaboration. It also means linking communities to related initiatives such as a corporate university.

One way to strengthen communities of practice is to provide them with official sponsors and support teams. Such sponsors and teams do not design the communities or prescribe their activities or outcomes. Instead, they work with internal community leaders to provide resources and coordination.

Companies have done this using a range of approaches. Compare the cases of two organizations—American Management Systems (AMS) and the World Bank—each of which has adopted the community of practice as the foundation of its knowledge management strategy. AMS takes an especially formal approach, while the World Bank combines formal and informal methods. A few years ago, AMS was going through an intense period of growth and globalization and, as a result, was losing its distinctive ability to leverage knowledge across the company. Then-chairman Charles Rossotti personally invited "thought leaders," who had been nominated by their business units, to spearhead the development of communities of practice in strategic areas. The company pays for two to three weeks of the leaders' time each year for these activities.

Community membership at AMS is a privilege. To join a community, a potential member must be recognized as an expert by his or her manager. Once on board, a participant has to complete one knowledge-development project per year—for instance, documenting a best practice—in order to remain in the community. Community members' participation is paid for by their business units, which fund their annual projects, cover their attendance at workshops, and send them to an annual conference that brings together all the company's communities of practice.

At the World Bank, president James Wolfensohn established the goal of making his organization the "knowledge bank"—a global source for high-quality information on economic development—so that it could better fulfill its mission of eradicating poverty. Key people throughout the organization then took the initiative to start communities of practice. Membership is open, and members decide on the level of participation that suits their needs. Communities of practice receive funding for specific activities and manage their own budgets.

At both AMS and the World Bank, senior management boards sponsor communities. Support teams help with community development and coordinate annual community conferences, knowledge fairs, library services, and technical support. Both organizations also have started to fund positions for knowledge managers who assist community leaders. These facilitators coordinate the groups, organize events, respond to queries from members, and keep the communities current on information from external sources.

AMS is exploring ways of explicitly rewarding community members. It has a promotion system that formally acknowledges their work, and it grants nonfinancial rewards such as early access to innovative technology and special business cards that attest to the members' expertise. The World Bank also formally recognizes community participation through its personnel evaluation system, but to drive participation it relies primarily on the intrinsic benefits of community membership: the opportunities to solve problems, develop new ideas, and build relationships with peers who share a common passion.

At both AMS and the World Bank, communities of practice have brought together people and ideas, and they have spread knowledge throughout the companies' global operations. They have made demonstrable and significant contributions to the organizations' goals. These two cases show how different styles of formal commitment to communities of practice by senior managers can be very effective when aligned with the organization's culture.

The best way for a senior executive to assess the value of a community of practice is by listening to members' stories in a systematic way.

USING NONTRADITIONAL METHODS TO MEASURE VALUE

Leaders intuitively recognize the benefit of developing people's capabilities. That said, most have difficulty understanding the value of communities. For one thing, the effects of community activities are often delayed. For another, results generally appear in the work of teams and business units, not in the communities themselves. And it's often hard to determine whether a great idea that surfaced during a community meeting would have bubbled up anyway in a different setting. Such complexity makes it very difficult for managers to assess the value of communities.

The best way for an executive to assess the value of a community of practice is by listening to members' stories, which can clarify the complex relationships among activities, knowledge, and performance. "The idea we pursued at that meeting helped me persuade the customer to continue to buy our service." "Thanks to advice from the community, I got done in two days what normally takes me two weeks." "I took a risk because I was confident I had the backing of my community—and it paid off."

The solution to the conundrum of valuing communities of practice is to gather anecdotal evidence systematically. You can't just collect certain stories, perhaps the most compelling ones, because isolated events can be unrepresentative. A systematic effort captures the diversity and range of activities that communities are involved in.

At Shell, community coordinators often conduct interviews to collect these stories and then publish them in newsletters and reports. AMS organizes a yearly competition to identify the best stories. An analysis of a sample of stories revealed that the communities had saved the company $2 million to $5 million and increased revenue by more than $13 million in one year.

The New Frontier

Communities of practice are emerging in companies that thrive on knowledge. The first step for managers now is to understand what these communities are and how they work. The second step is to realize that they are the hidden fountainhead of knowledge development and therefore the key to the challenge of the knowledge economy. The third step is to appreciate the paradox that these informal structures require specific managerial efforts to develop them and to integrate them into the organization so that their full power can be leveraged.

Communities of practice are the new frontier. They

may seem unfamiliar now, but in five to ten years they may be as common to discussions about organization as business units and teams are today—if managers learn how to make them a central part of their companies' success.

Communities in Action

COMMUNITIES OF PRACTICE add value to organizations in several important ways:

They help drive strategy. Communities of practice are the heart and soul of the World Bank's knowledge management strategy. Some communities of practice have existed for years at the bank, but they were mostly small and fragmented. That has changed now that the bank has made knowledge management the key to its goal of becoming the "knowledge bank"—providing high-quality information and know-how about economic development.

The bank's decision to fund communities of practice, for example, led to a significant increase in the number of organizationwide communities—it's now over 100—and in the intensity of participation. As the bank supplements its emphasis on lending money with providing development expertise, these communities will increasingly contribute to the bank's strategic direction.

They start new lines of business. Consider how a group of consultants from one firm created a community that eventually generated an entirely new line of business. The group met regularly at O'Hare airport between engagements with clients. Its domain was retail marketing in the banking industry, and the meetings focused on new business opportunities for clients. Over a two-year period, the initial group of five to seven consultants attracted many others within the firm. Four years after the first meeting, the community had created a new line of marketing approaches for financial services companies. And it convened 200 people from the firm in New Orleans for its annual conference. The community acted like a petri dish for entrepreneurial insights that ultimately generated more clients, shaped the firm's strategy, and enhanced its reputation.

They solve problems quickly. Members of a community of practice know whom to ask for help with a problem. They also know how to ask questions so that peers can quickly comprehend and focus on the heart of the problem. At Buckman Labs, members of communities of practice from around the world routinely respond to practice-specific queries within 24 hours. In one case, an employee trying to help a pulp mill customer in the Pacific Northwest solve a dye-retention problem received several responses within a day from expert peers in Europe, South Africa, and Canada—and one response provided exactly the solution the customer needed.

They transfer best practices. A community of practice does much more than work on specific problems. It's also an ideal forum for sharing and spreading best practices across a company.

Consider how the former Chrysler made this work, beginning in the early 1990s when the company broke up its functional departments to organize around car platforms such as small cars and minivans. Chrysler's leaders feared they would lose functional expertise and the ability to keep up with leading-edge change. To address those concerns, senior managers and engineers formed communities of practice known as "tech clubs," which were composed of experts from different car platforms. The clubs helped the company successfully make the move to platforms, a change that cut R&D costs and car-development cycle times by more than half.

Today the tech clubs are an important part of the integration of DaimlerChrysler. The clubs meet regularly to discuss questions in 11 areas of product development, including body design, electronics, and vehicle development. They analyze variations in practice and set standards. Engineers who participate in the clubs are responsible for developing and maintaining an Engineering Book of Knowledge, a database that captures information on compliance standards, supplier specifications, and best practices.

They develop professional skills. Studies have shown that apprentices learn as much from journeymen and more advanced apprentices as they do from master craftsmen. It seems clear, then, that effective learning depends on the availability of peers and their willingness to act as mentors and coaches. That applies not only to the education of inexperienced workers but also to that of experts. The best neurosurgeons don't rely simply on their own brilliance; they read peer-reviewed journals, attend conferences in which their colleagues discuss new research, and travel great distances to work alongside surgeons who are developing innovative techniques.

Some companies have found that communities of practice are particularly effective arenas for fostering professional development. At IBM, communities of practice hold their own conferences, both in person and online. Presentations, hallway conversations, dinners, and chat rooms are opportunities for members to exchange ideas, build skills, and develop networks.

They help companies recruit and retain talent. American Management Systems has found that communities of practice help the company win the war (or at least some of the battles) for talent. Thus a consultant who was planning to leave the company decided to stay after peers at a community forum found project opportunities for her that were tailor-made to her interests and expertise. Other valuable consultants—at least six, by one manager's count—stayed with the company after being invited to join a prestigious community of practice that would enable them to develop skills and find new clients.

Originally published in January–February 2000
Reprint R00110

The Smart-Talk Trap

JEFFREY PFEFFER AND ROBERT I. SUTTON

Executive Summary

IN TODAY'S BUSINESS WORLD, there's no shortage of know-how. When companies get into trouble, their executives have vast resources at their disposal: their own experiences, colleagues' ideas, reams of computer-generated data, thousands of publications, and consultants armed with the latest managerial concepts and tools.

But all too often, even with all that knowledge floating around, companies are plagued with an inertia that comes from knowing too much and doing too little—a phenomenon the authors call the *knowing-doing gap*.

The gap often can be traced to a basic human propensity: the willingness to let talk substitute for action. When confronted with a problem, people act as though discussing it, formulating decisions, and hashing out plans for action are the same as actually fixing it.

21

And after researching organizations of all shapes and sizes, the authors concluded that a particular kind of talk is an especially insidious inhibitor of action: "smart talk." People who can engage in such talk generally sound confident and articulate; they can spout facts and may even have interesting ideas. But such people often exhibit the less benign aspects of smart talk as well: They focus on the negative, and they favor unnecessarily complex or abstract language. The former lapses into criticism for criticism's sake; the latter confuses people. Both tendencies can stop action in its tracks.

How can you shut the smart-talk trap and close the knowing-doing gap? The authors lay out five methods that successful companies employ in order to translate the right kind of talk into intelligent action.

CONSIDER TWO STORIES, both sadly true and sadly typical.

- An international metals and oil company was posting terrible numbers—sales and profits were down, as was share price. The company's senior executives were mortified by the results; they knew major changes in strategy and operations were imperative. Their response: to spend at least half their time in darkened rooms, watching elaborate presentations about the company's performance.

- Faced with a worrisomely slow time-to-market for its new products, a large furniture company conducted a careful benchmarking study. The results were clear: a project-based organizational structure would help solve the problem. But more than a year later, the company had not instituted a single change. Senior executives, although uniformly supportive of the idea of restructuring the organization, were still discussing it in meetings that ended with . . . decisions to have more meetings.

At the center of both stories is a particular kind of inertia that plagues companies of every size and type. In our four years of research at nearly 100 companies, we observed it at global conglomerates and at 20-employee start-ups, at capital-intensive manufacturers and at knowledge-driven service firms. It is not the inertia of indifference or ignorance but of knowing too much and doing too little. We call this phenomenon the *knowing-doing gap.*

Most executives know what they should do when their companies get into trouble—when sales slip or customer satisfaction erodes or productivity and quality problems emerge. To plot a course, they can draw on their own experience and insight, their colleagues' ideas, and the reams of data produced by sophisticated information systems. If that's not enough, they can tap into the myriad resources that exist outside the walls of their own companies—the 1,700 business books and thousands of articles published every year, the legions of management consultants armed with the latest tools and concepts, the dozens of gurus making the rounds on the speaking circuit. In today's business world, there is no shortage of know-how.

But all too often, even with all that knowledge floating around, nothing happens. There's no *doing*. Yes, some companies are adept at translating ideas into action. A handful are even famous for it, such as General Electric,

IDEO Product Development, and AES Corporation. But they are the exceptions. Most organizations have trouble bridging the knowing-doing gap. Brought to a standstill by inertia, their problems fester, their opportunities for growth are lost, and their best employees become frustrated and leave. If the inactivity continues, customers and investors react accordingly and take their money elsewhere.

What causes the knowing-doing gap? It can often be traced to a basic human propensity: the willingness to let talk substitute for action. "Between the conception / And the creation / Falls the shadow," T.S. Eliot wrote in "The Hollow Men," his great poem about human inertia. In business, that shadow is composed of words. When confronted with a problem, people act as if discussing it, formulating decisions, and hashing out plans for action are the same as actually fixing it. It's an understandable response—after all, talk, unlike action, carries little risk. But it can paralyze a company.

That's exactly what Xerox discovered in the 1980s, when the company's executives decided that quality improvements were necessary to bring down costs and raise customer satisfaction. Over the next four years, employees at every level attended an almost endless series of meetings and off-site conferences to discuss the quality initiative. About 70,000 employees received six days of training each, and executives created a 92-page book of implementation guidelines.

But all that talking was just hot air. In 1989, a Harvard Business School case study on the project revealed that there had been very little change in the attitudes of Xerox's managers toward quality. Few concrete decisions had been made to change the quality of the company's products. Nor had beliefs and behaviors been altered. For instance, only 15% of Xerox employees said they believed that recognition and rewards were based on improvements in quality, and only 13% reported using cost-of-quality analyses in their decision making.

Meaningful action occurred only when Xerox was required to document concrete quality improvements—and the managerial processes that led to them—as part of its application for the Malcolm Baldrige Quality Award. The company's Business Products and Systems division then went into overdrive to implement change and eventually won the award. But who knows how many growth opportunities had passed the company by during the years of empty talk? (For another example of the knowing-doing gap at work, see "The Empty Words of Mission Statements" at the end of this article.)

We found that a particular kind of talk is an especially insidious inhibitor of organizational action: "smart talk." The elements of smart talk include sounding confident, articulate, and eloquent; having interesting information and ideas; and possessing a good vocabulary. But smart talk tends to have other, less benign components: first, it focuses on the negative, and second, it is unnecessarily complicated or abstract (or both). In other words, people engage in smart talk to spout criticisms and complexities. Unfortunately, such talk has an uncanny way of stopping action in its tracks. That's why we call this dynamic the *smart-talk trap*.

Why Talk Prevails

Managers let talk substitute for action because that's what they've been trained to do. Many executives in contemporary organizations have been to business school, and even those who don't have M.B.A. degrees often attend executive education programs taught by business school faculty. What do they learn in those programs? That the ability to talk—and particularly to talk smart— pays.

Smart talk is the essence of management education at leading institutions in the United States and throughout the world. Students learn how to sound smart in class- room discussions and how to write smart things on essay examinations. A substantial part of students' grades is usually based on how much they say and how smart they sound in class. As Robert Reid recounts in his book, *Year One: An Intimate Look Inside Harvard Business School:* "My general concern about class participation increased throughout the week. . . . My urgency was heightened by the fact that grades (and First-Year Honors! And McKin- sey! . . .) depended so heavily on in-class commentary. . . . The opportunity to speak was such a precious commod- ity that most people were terrified about blowing it by saying something shallow, repetitive, or. . . stupid when they were finally called on."

Grading students on class participation makes peda- gogical sense. It encourages them to think carefully about what they are reading. But telling students that they must sound smart in order to succeed has a pernicious effect as well. They learn that they need only to deliver an intelli- gent insight—or an intelligent critique of someone else's insight—to impress their professors. They don't actually have to implement the recommendations or act on the insights that emerge in the conversation.

Compare business education with the training people receive when their performance is a matter of life or death. Soldiers, pilots, and surgeons all receive classroom training, of course, but it quickly turns into learning by doing. The military requires soldiers to perform the very maneuvers that will be necessary during wartime. Pilots get into the cockpit and take off. In surgery, there is an old saying that describes how residents learn a procedure: "Hear one, see one, do one." In business education, the saying would go, "Hear one, talk about one, talk about one some more."

Once in the workplace, business school graduates continue to be rewarded for talking. The value of smart talk is particularly reflected, and reinforced, in one of their most popular career choices: management consulting. (See "The Price—and Value—of Advice" at the end of this article.) But even in traditional nuts-and-bolts industries and high-tech start-ups, talk carries currency. Because management today revolves around meetings, teams, and consensus building, the more a person says, the more valuable he or she appears. Our observations of contemporary organizations show that people who talk frequently are more likely to be judged by others as influential and important—they're considered leaders. We once asked a new division manager why she had been selected for the job over several others. "They gave me the job because I couldn't keep my mouth shut and wouldn't let anyone else say anything," she answered with a laugh, "and now that I'm the boss, they expect me to talk even more than before."

The manager's implicit theory—although said in jest—is supported by numerous organizational and anthropological studies. The studies all suggest that some people talk more than others in order to come out on top in a group's "conversational marketplace." The research also supports what Bernard Bass, in the classic summary of scholarly studies on leadership, *Bass and Stogdill's Handbook of Leadership*, has called the "babble" or "blabbermouth" theory of leadership. The theory states that people who talk more often and longer—regardless of the quality of their comments—are more likely to emerge as leaders of new groups, to be identified as leaders by observers of the group, to be viewed as influential by both group members and outsiders, and to have greater influence on group decisions.

People who want to get ahead in organizations learn that talking a lot helps them reach their goal more reliably than taking action or inspiring others to act does. And once people reach the heights, they are expected to talk more than ever. By dominating the group's "air-time," they let everyone know who's in charge.

There's another reason why talk—and especially smart talk—is so highly rewarded in organizations. Executives are constantly required to make important decisions about whom to hire, fire, promote, and assign to particular tasks. They often make those decisions based on limited information about the individuals in question. That's because in large, complex companies, they can't really know what every person has accomplished. It's just not visible. The organization's performance comes from the actions of many interdependent people, so discerning any one person's contribution is fraught with the potential for error. Moreover, people switch jobs so often these days that it is often hard to assess precisely what they have done.

What an executive can know more easily is how smart a person sounds. That information is easily accessible through routine meetings, presentations, and everyday conversations. Of course, it is also incomplete, but that's beside the point—it's right there for executives to observe and judge. In fact, at least three research studies—conducted by psychologists from the late 1950s through the early 1980s—demonstrated that interviewers made up their minds about job candidates within the first minutes of a conversation. The judgments were based on candidates' perceived intelligence—that is, on how smart they sounded.

The fact that people get hired, promoted, and assigned to coveted jobs based on their ability to sound intelligent, and not necessarily on their ability to act that way, is well known in most organizations. People have seen it happen all too often. The received message is: Don't worry about your accomplishments, just make sure you sound good. That message doesn't inspire people to leap into action—it often has the opposite effect. And thus the knowing-doing gap widens.

Criticism and Complexity

It is difficult, perhaps, to blame people for using smart talk to do well in school or to move up the career ladder. Likewise, one can sympathize with an overwhelmed executive in a large global company who may be overly impressed with a job candidate's ability to sound smart. But the more negative components of smart talk—the tendency to tear an idea down without offering anything positive in its place, and the belief that complex language and ideas are somehow better than simple ones—cannot be rationalized so easily.

At a global financial institution we studied, junior executives made a point—especially in meetings with their bosses present—of trashing the ideas of their peers. Every time someone dared to offer an idea, everyone around the table would leap in with reasons why it was nothing short of idiotic. Senior executives didn't try to stop the verbal fray. Sometimes they even nodded approvingly as smart-sounding faultfinders critiqued ideas to death.

The evidence that being critical of others makes a person appear smarter is not just anecdotal. Teresa Amabile, a professor at Harvard Business School, confirmed the point in a 1983 study called "Brilliant but Cruel." Amabile found that people who wrote negative book reviews were perceived by others as being less likable but more intelligent, competent, and expert than people who wrote positive reviews of the same books. She summarized her findings by noting, "Only pessimism sounds profound. Optimism sounds superficial."

People will try to sound smart not only by being critical but also by using trendy, pretentious language.

So true—and so easy to connect to the knowing-doing gap. If those with the courage to propose something concrete have been devastated in the process, they'll either leave or learn to be smart-talkers themselves. As a result, a company will end up being filled with clever put-down artists. It will also end up paralyzed by the fear and silence those people spawn.

People will try to sound smart not only by being critical but also by using trendy, pretentious, or overblown language. Take the case of a software company that gave its employees laptop computers to provide them with access to e-mail and the Internet at home. Its executives described the initiative as a "transformation to a virtual organization." The jargon led people to believe the laptops were part of a massive reorganization. That resulted in scary rumors—"Our office is closing and we're all going to have to work from our homes." In reality, the executives wanted employees to use new technology to make their working lives more flexible. It took them several weeks to quell the rumors and get people focused on their work again. By using fancy language to describe a simple plan, the executives lost people's trust and slowed the adoption of the e-mail system.

Sometimes managers themselves don't know what they're talking about when they use complex language, as we discovered when we asked a number of them to define some of the terms they used frequently—such as "learning organization," "business process reengineering," "chaos theory," and "paradigm." In many instances, the executives couldn't offer any definition at all, or if they gave one, it was woefully vague. Imagine the chilling effect such confusion might cause. It is hard enough to explain how to put a complex idea into practice when you understand the idea. It is impossible when you don't.

Rare is the manager who presents a new strategy with a single slide and an idea that can be summarized in a sentence.

Executives don't just pepper their talk with complex language, they also latch on to complex concepts with great gusto. Rare is the manager who stands before his or her peers to present a new strategy with a single slide and an idea that can be summarized in a sentence or two. Instead, managers congratulate themselves and one another when they come up with ideas that are so elaborate and convoluted they require two hours of multipart, multicolored slides and a liberal sprinkling of the latest buzzwords.

The common rationale for complex concepts does, on the surface, appear to make sense. It is as follows: In order to thrive, companies must develop a sustainable competitive advantage, which requires doing something that is difficult to imitate. It is harder to imitate complex strategies and the management systems that go with them than it is to copy simple ones. Thus competitive advantage is built by doing complicated things. A corollary is that simple prescriptions are not of much value. After all, if simple ideas really worked, everyone would already be using them. The same logic applies to old ideas. Surely if old ideas could help companies, they would be put into practice everywhere. The conclusion is this: only rare and complex concepts are worth adopting.

But while it's true that sustainable competitive advantage is built by doing things that are difficult to imitate, complex strategies are not the only ones that are hard to copy. Ease of comprehension should never be mixed up with ease of implementation. "Simple" strategies can be tough to implement—and thus imitate. Take three straightforward practices: decentralization, information sharing, and treating people with respect. Decentralization requires managers to give up decision-making power, which is one of the hardest feats they can be asked to perform. Similarly, information sharing entails giving up the power and prestige that come from knowing things that others don't. And thousands of companies prove the point that treating people with respect, although easy to talk about and easy to grasp conceptually, is difficult to put into practice.

We're not claiming that complex language and concepts never add value to an organization. We are saying that they bring a lot less value than most executives realize. In our research, we observed that the most common reaction to complexity was confusion. And it's an unusual company that can act effectively when its people are confused.

Shutting the Trap, Closing the Gap

We're not arguing for an end to conversations, meetings, or presentations, or that people should stop trying to sound smart. The right kind of talk can inspire and guide intelligent action. It's just that talk can't be allowed to become a substitute for action. Fortunately, not all organizations are plagued by the knowing-doing gap. Some have managed to avoid the smart-talk trap. In those companies, people consistently say smart things, then do them. What typifies such organizations? Our research suggests that they share five characteristics.

THEY HAVE LEADERS WHO KNOW AND DO THE WORK

Companies that use talk productively—that is, to guide and spur action—are usually led by people who have an intimate knowledge of the organization's people, products, and processes. Such leaders are frequently home-grown, but even if they aren't, they make it a priority to learn and do the work, take part in teams, serve customers, and oversee manufacturing operations. Take James Goodnight, CEO of SAS Institute, a $750 million software company that has experienced 22 years of double-digit growth. Goodnight spends 40% of his time programming software and leading product development teams. You are just as likely to find him in an R&D building as in his office. Similarly, at Men's Wearhouse, a successful chain of more than 400 outlets, CEO George Zimmer and other senior executives regularly visit their stores. Regional and district managers also spend time on the floor, coaching salespeople and talking with customers.

Leaders who do the work, rather than just talk about it, help prevent the knowing-doing gap from opening in the first place. Working on the front lines keeps them in touch with the organization's real capabilities and challenges; that experience allows them to play a critical role in turning knowledge into action. Goodnight, for example, thoroughly understands SAS's emerging technologies and daunting scheduling demands. His firsthand experience showed him that when exhausted people try to program software, they make more errors. That insight led him to set the company's workweek at 35 hours, with two results: first, SAS needs fewer programming checkers (which saves money), and second, it releases software with fewer bugs (which keeps customers happy).

Equally important, because they are intimately familiar with the real work of the organization, such executives are less likely to be taken in by fancy words and complex plans that are fancy and complex for their own sake. It would be impossible, for instance, for an SAS executive to sell Goodnight on a complicated plan to accelerate the company's production schedule without also providing a solid assessment of manpower requirements and a cost-benefit analysis that rang true. Likewise, no one at Men's Wearhouse could convince Zimmer to approve a "promising" new training program or marketing campaign that was riddled with implementation problems. Leaders who know and do the work can cut through the smart talk.

THEY HAVE A BIAS FOR PLAIN LANGUAGE AND SIMPLE CONCEPTS

Companies that avoid the knowing-doing gap are often masters of the mundane. Executives devote their efforts to a few straightforward priorities that have clear implications for action. These organizations realize the value of direct language and understandable concepts. They consider "common sense" a compliment rather than an insult.

When Greg Brennemen, president and COO of Continental Airlines, led the turnaround that improved the company's on-time performance from worst to first in one year, he used a shockingly simple plan. He rebuilt relations with the employees who actually kept the planes going and served the customers, and he emphasized the need to provide better customer service and to fly on time. Brennemen's straightforward plan worked better than the several elaborate multimillion-dollar bailout attempts that preceded it.

Plain talk and simple concepts are valuable because they are more likely to lead to action. You may disagree with a simple plan, but you can't claim confusion as an excuse to ignore it. Plain talk and simple concepts are marching orders.

A case in point is Apple Computer. When Steve Jobs took over in July 1997, Apple's computer platforms included the 1400, 2400, 3400, 4400, 5400, 5500, 6500, 7300, 7600, 8600, 9600, the 20th-Anniversary Mac, e-Mate, Newton, and the Pippin. After listening to insiders explain the product line to him for three weeks, Jobs said, "I couldn't figure it out. We couldn't even tell our friends which one to buy." The complexity not only confused customers, it also meant that people inside Apple were often unsure about where to focus their product-development and marketing efforts. And it gummed up production.

Jobs quickly decided that Apple could meet the needs of its customers with "four great products." Next, he got the clear message out: Apple would make one product in each category—business desktops, business portables, consumer desktops, and consumer portables—and would discontinue everything else. After two years of "working like crazy, trying like crazy just to do that,"

Apple has the hottest-selling computer in the land, the iMac, and has returned to profitability.

THEY FRAME QUESTIONS BY ASKING "HOW," NOT JUST "WHY."

In companies where a culture of criticism flourishes, few people are willing to proffer ideas, and even fewer have the guts to throw themselves into action. Failure always brings a chorus of "I told you so" from the put-down artists, who, by the way, rarely allow themselves to face the firing line by taking on a project that requires real work.

Some companies, however, prevent a culture of criticism from developing by having informal rules about the way ideas are analyzed. People are permitted to raise objections to plans and concepts, but they can't just ask, "Why would we do such a thing?" Instead, they must suggest how it would be possible to surmount the obstacles they foresee. In other words, the conversation focuses not on faults but on overcoming them.

Donald Regan was a master of framing "how" questions. Regan ran Merrill Lynch in the 1970s, just as financial service companies were confronted with the invention of the cash management account (CMA), which linked checking accounts, credit cards, money market funds, and traditional brokerage services. Although CMAs are now common, in the 1970s they were a tremendous innovation and promised Merrill Lynch a competitive advantage if it could exploit them on a large scale.

Regan hired the consulting firm SRI to help Merrill Lynch assess the implications of entering the CMA market. After a three-month study, the consultants presented a strongly positive report to Regan and his top team. An executive who was there recalled what happened next:

"Regan went around the room getting comments from the other senior executives. They all saw problems. The operations vice president noted that it now cost the firm many dollars to process a transaction. That was fine when the transactions were securities purchases and sales, for which the commissions were large. But when the transactions were deposits in money market accounts or checks written on such accounts, the company would have to be able to process them for only cents per transaction. The systems simply were not able to handle the task. Then the legal vice president noted that the CMA ideas would in effect turn the firm into a bank, making it subject to much more stringent regulation. It would have to go through the difficult process of obtaining charters and regulatory approvals. And the marketing vice president noted that banks were currently some of Merrill Lynch's best customers. They would certainly be offended if the firm became a competitor and might take much of their business to other securities firms."

Regan did not dismiss the problems. After all, they were genuine and difficult barriers to implementation. But he said that he had decided to proceed because of the importance of the product to the company. Then he asked, "The question is, How do we solve the problems you described so articulately?"

The story about Regan underscores an organizational reality. There will always be discussion in companies, but executives have it in their power to determine its character. People can use their voices either to find fault or to find fault and then fix it.

THEY HAVE STRONG MECHANISMS THAT CLOSE THE LOOP

Not all talk is aimless, of course. Sometimes it does lead to a decision to take action. But at companies that suffer from the knowing-doing gap, the process ends with the decision. The companies in our study that bridged the gap, however, had effective mechanisms in place to make sure decisions didn't just end on paper but actually got implemented.

The mechanisms come in many and varied forms. At Cypress Semiconductor, for instance, when people commit to do something by a certain date, that information is entered into the company's computer system. If they fail to meet the deadline, they may find that their computers don't work. Other companies routinely assign specific people the responsibility of ensuring that decisions get turned into action; those people are held accountable for reporting on results at a meeting with executives. At still other companies, no meeting ends without a written record of who is going to do what by when; that record is then circulated or posted for all to see. Such peer pressure can be a remarkably powerful impetus for action.

Closing the loop—following up to make sure something actually happens after it has been decided on—isn't a very complicated idea. But it is a potent means for preventing talk from being the only thing that occurs.

THEY BELIEVE THAT EXPERIENCE IS THE BEST TEACHER

Finally, companies that elude the knowing-doing gap follow a very out-of-fashion practice in this age of seminars, training programs, instructional CD-ROMs, and distance learning. They make the process of doing into an opportunity to learn. Sometimes they even leap into a project before they are completely sure it will work, just to learn from the experience. Or they launch initiatives before every last detail is ironed out. How daring—and how smart!

At IDEO Product Development, one of the largest and most successful product-design consulting firms in the world, CEO David Kelley likes to say that "enlightened trial and error outperforms the planning of flawless intellects." IDEO believes in building prototypes—not fancy or expensive prototypes, but models that will permit its engineers to learn something. Its headquarters are filled with models, toys, and gizmos that help people think creatively about design and technology, initially on a small scale. Says engineer Peter Skillman, "Rapid prototyping is our religion. When we get an idea, we make it right away so we can see it, try it, and learn from it." The company also believes in "failing early and failing often"— which is sensible when you consider that the alternative is to fail late and fail big.

The dramatic turnaround of Bayport Terminal in Seabrook, Texas, is another case that demonstrates the benefits of using action as a teacher. Before 1994, the terminal, operated at the time by the chemical group of Hoechst Celanese Corporation, loaded nearly 3 billion pounds of chemicals per year into drums and onto ships, barges, and trucks. Then Annette Kyle became its manager.

Kyle quickly discovered that most of the practices used at the terminal were the same as they had always been, even though the volume of material it handled had increased dramatically since it opened in 1974. The terminal was enormously inefficient. For instance, it was paying about $2.5 million a year in demurrage fees. (The company running the dock pays such fees to a ship when it is unready to load or unload that ship immediately upon its arrival. While the ship waits, the penalty is about $10,000 per hour.) Kyle was also troubled to find that it took people at the terminal an average of three hours to load a truck, even though the industry average was less than one.

After Kyle had spent a year learning the ropes, she and her staff orchestrated a revolution at the terminal to address those problems. Rather than talk, they plunged into action. In a period of just a few days, they made sweeping changes. They eliminated direct supervisors, assigned areas of responsibility, installed self-managing teams, and implemented metrics that allowed every employee to see how well the terminal was keeping pace with the work.

The positive effects of the change were evident almost immediately. Demurrage fees dropped from more than $1 million in the first half of 1995 to less than $10,000 in the first half of 1996. Also in the first half of that year, more than 90% of the trucks were loaded within an hour of their arrival. Although the employees were shocked by the changes at first, they soon learned—by doing—new and better ways of working. And according to employee attitude surveys conducted by independent researchers in May 1996, they were highly satisfied with those changes.

Interestingly, one of the reasons Kyle's revolution suc-ceeded was because it was reinforced by the practice of framing questions with "how" in addition to "why." Kyle believed that one of the biggest barriers to change was that people constantly whined about things but didn't take responsibility for making them better. She had "No

Whining" patches sewn on everyone's uniform and explained that complaining about something without trying to do anything about it was not acceptable. If employees found something wrong, it was their job to fix the problem. And if they couldn't fix it, they were to bring the problem to Kyle or to another team leader, who would then be responsible for doing everything possible to fix it.

The Bayport Terminal story is a good example of how the five practices that mitigate the knowing-doing gap reinforce one another. To begin with, Kyle understood the work that was done at the terminal; she spent a year learning its functions and becoming familiar with people before launching her revolution. Once the transformation was under way, she explained its purpose in clear, simple language, and she recast discussions to focus on solving problems, not simply on identifying them. As for closing the loop, Kyle instituted the regular practice of gathering and publishing company performance figures.

The Rewards of Action

In the course of our research into the knowing-doing gap, we met a consultant who was making a proposal to a large U.S. bank that was in good financial shape but wanted to do better. The consultant told us that as he and his team of eager colleagues put their proposal together from data provided by the bank, they came upon reports assembled for the bank by four other consulting firms over the past six years. The recommendations were identical. Why, asked the consultant, would anyone pay for the same answer five times? How crazy is that?

Very. But it is also altogether common. Business-people love to talk, which is fine when it leads to action. When it becomes a substitute for getting things done, shareholders, customers, and employees pay a price— and often executives do, too. The simple fact is, you can't take words to the bank, no matter how smart they sound. But when you close the knowing-doing gap, you discover the rewards of action.

The Empty Words of Mission Statements

MISSION STATEMENTS PROVIDE a familiar example of how executives allow talk to substitute for action. Several securities firms and investment banks we studied had spent long hours crafting elegant mission statements that extolled the values of teamwork, integrity, and respect for the individual. But partners at those firms treated their young analysts like short-term contractors. They not only gave them work that wasn't commensurate with their skills but also were often openly impolite and even abusive.

When we mentioned that to the leaders of one of the investment banks, they reacted with incredulity. Disrespectful behavior was precluded by their mission statement, they said—it couldn't be happening. But it was, because the managers had let a plaque on the wall substitute for action. The executives assumed that saying something made it so. Reality, however, proved that merely saying something guarantees nothing. When it comes to mission statements, it is often as Eileen Shapiro suggests in her book, *Fad Surfing in the Boardroom*: they are little more than "a talisman, hung in public places, to ward off evil spirits."

Sometimes they don't even do that.

The Price—and Value—of Advice

HAVING LEARNED THAT smart talk brings good grades, many business students throng to strategy consulting, where they discover that smart talk brings big bucks as well. What, after all, do consultants do? More to the point, what is their output? Reports and presentations filled with sharp-looking overheads!

That is not to discount the value that consultants can add. Some firms offer their clients rare and useful insights on the macroeconomy. Others offer industry expertise, best practices in systematic data gathering, or valuable new perspectives on old problems.

What they don't provide is implementation. While many strategy consulting companies now claim that they specialize in implementation, most remain firmly entrenched in the business of providing advice and make only an occasional foray into putting that advice into action. (To be fair, consultants might like to make more forays: they routinely complain that their reports and presentations do not lead to organizational action.)

If you're a young business school grad, the consulting life is certainly attractive from a monetary standpoint. You can go into industry, become a plant manager, and make maybe $80,000 or $100,000 a year. Or you can go into the business of talking to the plant manager and make about twice as much. The difference in dollars

not only sways career choices, it also sends a clear message about the value the economy places on being able
to run something versus being able to talk about running
something. The knowing-doing gap reflects that message. People know it makes sense—and cents—to know
rather than to do.

Originally published in May–June 1999
Reprint 99310

Balancing Act

How to Capture Knowledge Without Killing It

JOHN SEELY BROWN AND PAUL DUGUID

Executive Summary

EVERYONE KNOWS THAT the way things are formally organized in most companies (their processes) is not the same as the way things are actually done (their practices). The difference between the two creates tension that can be very difficult for managers to handle. Lean too much toward practice and new ideas may bubble up and evaporate for lack of a structure to harness them. Lean too much toward process and you may get no new ideas at all. The goal, then, is to tap into the creativity at work in every layer of an organization with a combination of process and practice.

Take, for example, the community of people who fix Xerox machines. Large machines, it turns out, are not as predictable as Xerox's documentation would suggest. So when following the service manual is not enough, the

45

reps come together—over breakfast, at breaks, at the end of the day—and talk about their own best practices. So far so good. But Xerox goes a step further. It has set up a process similar to an academic peer-review system to gather, vet, and share those best practices across the company. The reps get much-welcome recognition for their creativity, and local best practices are deployed companywide.

Dot-com companies are a hotbed of innovative practices. But as they mature, they, like Xerox, may find that they need seasoned managers who can harness those practices through the judicious application of constructive processes.

Top-down processes designed to institutionalize new ideas can gave a chilling effect on creativity. But they don't have to. Managers can learn to walk the fine line between rigidity—which smothers creativity—and chaos—where creativity runs amok and nothing gets to market.

History will pity the managers of the 1990s. The Internet touched down in their midst like a tornado, tearing up the old game book, disrupting every aspect of business, and compelling them to manage for a new economy. When managers sought help, they found the experts were offering two radically different theories about what such management should look like. The first approach—reengineering—focused on process. Organizations that reengineered their business processes would gain sustainable competitive advantage, according to an army of highly paid consultants. Major corporations spent millions of dollars and man-hours trying to do exactly that. But just as scores of reengineering VPs took their seats at *Fortune* 500 companies, word came down that process was stale. The *new* new thing was knowledge management—businesses that could capture the knowledge embedded in their organizations would own the future.

Reengineering and knowledge management are profoundly different approaches—as all those businesspeople who got whiplash from the turnaround soon realized. Reengineering is about the structured coordination of people and information. It's top-down. It assumes that it's easy to codify value creation. And it assumes that organizations compete in a predictable environment. Knowledge management focuses on effectiveness more than efficiency. It's bottom up. It assumes that managers can best foster knowledge by responding to the inventive, improvisational ways people actually get things done. It assumes that value-creating activities are not easy to pin down. And it assumes that organizations compete in an unpredictable environment.

Of course, management fads shift all the time. (How else could consultants stay in business?) But we think this shift from process engineering to knowledge management represents something more substantial than a change of fashion. It suggests a dilemma that all managers grapple with: the organizational tension between process, the way matters are formally organized, and practice, the way things actually get done.

Managers find this tension difficult to handle. They're paid to resolve or overcome tensions, but this is one they have to live with. Successful companies are not those that work around the problem; they are those that turn it to their advantage. For in the delicate art of balancing practice and process lies the means both to *foster* invention—by allowing new ideas to spark—and to *further* it—by implementing those same ideas. (See the exhibit, "Process Versus Practice.")

It's undoubtedly a hard balancing act. Lean too much toward practice, and you may get new ideas bubbling up all over the place, but you'll lack the structure to harness them. (And in the modern business world, worthwhile ideas that you don't harness end up in your competitors' hands.) Lean too much toward process, and you get lots of structure but too little freedom of movement to strike that initial spark. Finding the right balance is a central task for managers everywhere. It's embodied in a million business fads, and it transcends them all.

It is possible to strike the right balance. In this article, we'll look closely at an example drawn from a company we know well because we work there. This is the story of how Xerox Corporation learned to foster best practice among a particular group of employees and then to circulate their expertise using the organizational support that process can provide.

Process vs. Practice

Process	Practice
The way tasks are organized	The way tasks are done
Routine	Spontaneous
Orchestrated	Improvised
Assumes a predictable environment	Responds to a changing, unpredictable environment
Relies on explicit knowledge	Driven by tacit knowledge
Linear	Weblike

The Limits of Process-Based Thinking

One way managers attempt to resolve the tension between process and practice is by compartmentalizing. They do everything possible to foster invention and creativity among highly paid, elite workers (designers and scientists, for example). At the same time, they try to make everyone else's work completely predictable and to hold the majority of workers tight within the clamps of process. As a result, searches for underutilized knowledge round up the usual suspects—the output of the obviously inventive—and ignore everyone else, whose work practices are thought of as purely routine.

But this compartmentalization doesn't reflect the way most businesses currently operate. Today even the people involved in seemingly routine work practices have to be inventive because the world they're working in changes so quickly. Their routines are always a little out of kilter. They must improvise to make up the difference between the conditions their routines were designed for and the actual conditions thrown up by a mutable world.

Consider an ordinary business form. Even the most recently printed (or Web-posted) form usually has boxes that are no longer used, categories that no longer apply. These redundant boxes are signposts of change. Employees quickly devise ways to fix the slightly out-of-date process. "Oh, leave that box," they'll tell customers, "but make sure to check under 'c.' That will ring a bell in the marketing department, and they'll take care of you."

This particular example is insignificant. But such conversations—which happen all the time—are evidence of practical inventiveness used to get around the limits of process. These small fixes may be part of a company's best practice—where local inventiveness has enabled practices on the ground to outstrip processes on paper. All the small, individually insignificant best practices scattered around a company add up to an enormous amount of knowledge.

For a company to make the most of that knowledge—to "know what it knows," in the famous phrase of former Hewlett-Packard CEO Lew Platt—it needs to take practice, practitioners, and the communities that practitioners form seriously. That requires two steps. First, managers need to learn what local knowledge exists. Then if the knowledge looks valuable, they need to put it into wider circulation. Let's take those tasks one at a time. They lie at the heart of knowledge management, of course, and they also show us a lot about the tension between process and practice.

Knowing What You Know

Identifying a company's best practices is not easy, for a couple of reasons. First, there's a large gap between what a task looks like in a process manual and what it looks like in reality. Second, there's a gap between what people think they do and what they really do. Actual work practices are full of tacit improvisations that the employees who carry them out would have trouble articulating. The manager who wishes to understand the company's best practices must bridge both of those gaps.

To illustrate the difficulty of identifying best practices, we'll look at the customer service representatives who fix Xerox machines. From the process perspective, a rep's work can be described quickly. Customers having difficulty call the Customer Service Center. The center, in turn, notifies a rep. He or she then goes to the customer's site. With the help of error codes, which report the machine's state, and documentation, which says what those codes mean, the rep diagnoses the problem and follows instructions for fixing it. Practice here would seem to involve little more than following the map you are given and doing whatever it tells you to do.

It would seem that way, if someone hadn't bothered to look more closely. Julian Orr, formerly an anthropologist at Xerox's Palo Alto Research Center (PARC), studied what reps actually did, not what they were assumed to do. And what they actually did turned out to be quite different from the process we've just described. The reps' work is organized by business processes, without a doubt. But they succeed primarily by departing from formal processes; those processes followed to the letter would soon bring their work (and their clients' work) to a halt.

For example, the company's documented repair processes assume that machines work predictably. Yet large machines, made up of multiple subsystems, are not so predictable. Each reflects the age and condition of its parts, the particular way it's used, and the environment in which it sits, which may be hot, cold, damp, dry, clean, dusty, secluded, in traffic, or otherwise.

What happens when the reps fall off the map? There's a simple answer to that question. When the path leads off the map, the reps go . . . to breakfast.

Any single machine may have profound idiosyncrasies. Reps know the machines they work with, Orr suggests, as shepherds know their sheep. While everyone else assumes one machine is like the next, a rep knows each by its peculiarities and sorts out general failings from particular ones.

Consequently, although the documentation gives the reps a map, the critical question for them is what to do when they fall off the map—which they do all the time. Orr found a simple answer to that question. When the path leads off the map, the reps go . . . to breakfast.

WHEN THE GOING GETS TOUGH

Orr began his account of the reps' day not where the process view begins—at nine o'clock, when the first call comes in—but at breakfast beforehand, where the reps share and even generate new insights into these difficult machines. Orr found that a quick breakfast can be worth hours of training. While eating, playing cribbage, and gossiping, the reps talked work, and talked it continually. They posed questions, raised problems, offered solutions, constructed answers, laughed at mistakes, and discussed changes in their work, the machines, and customer relations. Both directly and indirectly, they kept one another up to date about what they knew, what they'd learned, and what they were doing.

The reps' group breakfast shows that work goes on that formal processes don't capture. But it shows more. It demonstrates that a job that seems highly independent on paper is in reality remarkably social. Reps get together not only at the parts drop and the customer service center but also on their own time for breakfast, at lunch, for coffee, or at the end of the day—and sometimes at all of those times. This sociability is not just a retreat from the loneliness of an isolating job. The constant chatting is similar to the background updating that goes on all the time in any ordinary work site.

There, too, chatting usually passes unnoticed unless someone objects to it as a waste of time. But it's not. Orr

showed that the reps use one another as their most critical resources. In the course of socializing, the reps
develop a collective pool of practical knowledge that any
one of them can draw upon. That pool transcends any
individual member's knowledge, and it certainly transcends the corporation's documentation. Each rep con-
tributes to the pool, drawing from his or her own particular strengths, which the others recognize and rely on.
Collectively, the local groups constitute a community of
practice. (For a detailed description, see Chapter 1 "Communities of Practice: The Organizational Frontier.")

STORYTELLING

Much of the knowledge that exists within working
groups like the one formed by our Xerox reps comes
from their war stories. The constant storytelling about
problems and solutions, about disasters and triumphs
over breakfast, lunch, and coffee serves a number of
overlapping purposes. Stories are good at presenting
things sequentially (this happened, then that). Stories
also present things causally (this happened because of
that). Thus stories are a powerful way to understand
what happened (the sequence of events) and why (the
causes and effects of those events). Storytelling is particularly useful for the reps, for whom "what" and "why" are
critical but often hard matters to discern.

We all tell stories this way. Economists tell stories in
their models. Scientists tell stories in their experiments.
Executives tell stories in their business plans (see
"Strategic Stories: How 3M Is Rewriting Business Planning," HBR May–June 1998). Storytelling helps us discover something new about the world. It allows us to
pass that discovery on to others. And finally, it helps the

people who share the story develop a common outlook. Orr found that war stories give the reps a shared framework for interpretation that allows them to collaborate even though the formal processes assume they are working independently.

IMPROVISATION

Not all of the reps' problems can be solved over breakfast or by storytelling alone. Experimentation and improvisation are essential, too. One day, Orr observed a rep working with a particularly difficult machine. It had been installed recently, but it had never worked satisfactorily. Each time it failed, it produced a different error message. Following the established process for each particular message—replacing or adjusting parts—didn't fix the overall problem. And collectively the messages made no sense.

Having reached his limits, the rep summoned a specialist. The specialist could not understand what was going on, either. So the two spent the afternoon cycling the machine again and again, waiting for its intermittent crashes and recording its state when it did. At the same time, they cycled stories about similar-looking problems round and round until they, too, crashed up against this particular machine. The afternoon resembled a series of alternating improvisational jazz solos, as each man took the lead, ran with it for a little while, then handed it off to the other, this all against the bass-line continuo of the rumbling machine.

In the course of this practice, the two gradually brought their separate ideas closer together toward a shared understanding of the machine. Eventually, late in the day, everything clicked. The machine's erratic behavior, the experience of the two technicians, and the stories they told finally formed a single, coherent account. They made sense of the machine and worked out how to fix it. And the solution quickly became part of the community lore, passed around for others in their group to use if they encountered the same problem.

As Orr's study shows, executives who want to identify and foster best practices must pay very close attention to the practices as they occur in reality rather than as they are represented in documentation or process designs. Otherwise, they will miss the tacit knowledge produced in improvisation, shared through storytelling, and embedded in the communities that form around those activities. Does that mean process has no importance in this context? Of course not. But the processes that support how people work should be deeply informed by how they already work—not imposed from above by process designers who imagine they understand the work better than they actually do. Armed with a sense of what really happens on the ground, it's possible to design processes that prompt improvisation rather than ones that are blindly prescriptive.

Spreading What You Know

People working in small groups develop very rich knowledge in practice, as we've seen. Assuming a company has correctly identified those practices and the tacit knowledge embedded within them, the question becomes, How can we spread that useful knowledge around? This is the point at which process becomes useful. Process—in the form of organizational coordination—can get that local knowledge into wider circulation.

Let's return to the Xerox reps. The group Orr studied included about a dozen people; the rep force worldwide currently numbers some 25,000. Locally generated fixes and insights circulated pretty efficiently within the small group but rarely made it beyond. So people in different groups spent time grappling with problems that had already been solved elsewhere. The reps as a whole still didn't know what some reps, as a group, knew.

The far-flung communities that made up the entire network of reps needed some organizational support to help them share local knowledge around the world. So Xerox initiated the Eureka project to oversee the knowledge dissemination. The project set out to create a database to preserve resourceful ideas over time and deliver them over space.

Often what one person thinks useful others find flaky, idiosyncratic, incoherent, redundant, or just plain stupid.

Do we hear a yawn? Databases are the most basic of knowledge management tools. They're also among the most ignored. Organizations fill their databases with useful tips and data, and nobody uses them. Why should another be any different? The answer in this case is that it's different because of how the data are judged to be useful.

Most such databases, like most business processes, are top-down creations. Managers fill them with what they think will be useful for the people they manage. And—surprise, surprise—the people usually don't find them so. Yet even when individuals fill databases with their own ideas of what's useful, they aren't much help either. Often what one person thinks useful others find flaky, idiosyncratic, incoherent, redundant, or just plain stupid. The more a database contains everyone's favorite idea, the more unusable it becomes.

The Eureka database was designed to get past that problem by establishing a process to help capture best practices. Reps, not the organization, supply the tips. But reps also vet the tips. A reps submits a suggestion first to a local expert on the topic. Together, they refine the tip. It's then submitted to a centralized review process, organized according to business units. Here reps and engineers again vet the tips, accepting some, rejecting others, eliminating duplicates, and calling in experts on the particular product line to resolve doubts and disputes. If a tip survives this process, it becomes available to reps around the world, who have access to the tips database over the Web. So reps using the system know that the tips—and the database as a whole—are relevant, reliable, and probably not redundant.

It's interesting to compare this method of circulating knowledge with the established practices and formal processes of the scientific community. The two methods are quite similar. Scientists, too, work in small, local groups. To circulate their ideas more widely, they also put those ideas through a well-established process of peer review. If accepted, the ideas are then published for others to see.

Most scientists don't get paid for scientific articles. Good articles do, however, earn them status among their peers. They become known and respected for careful work, reliable results, and important insights. The reps have followed a similar course. The corporation offered to pay for the tips, but the pilot group of reps who helped design the system thought that would be a mistake, worrying, among other things, that payment for submissions would lead people to focus on quantity rather than quality in making submissions. Instead, the reps chose to have their names attached to tips. Those who submit good tips earn positive recognition. Because even good tips vary in quality, reps, like scientists, build social capital through the quality of their input. At a recent meeting of Xerox reps in Canada, one individual was surprised by a spontaneous standing ovation from coworkers who were expressing their respect for his tips. Of course, as in the scientific community, such recognition may also lead to career advancement. But it is important not to underestimate the value of social and intellectual capital within workplace communities—particularly those not usually recognized for their knowledge production.

The current Eureka database holds about 30,000 records. And its value is growing as it grows. In one case, an engineer in Brazil was about to replace a problematic high-end color machine (at a cost of about $40,000) for a disgruntled customer. Experimenting with a prototype of Eureka, he found a tip from a Montreal technician that led him to replace a defective 50 cent fuse instead. In all, Eureka is estimated to have saved the corporation $100 million.

Process and practice, then, do not represent rival views of the organization. Rather, they reflect the creative tension at the center of innovative organizations. In this, organizations resemble the well-known picture that, looked at once, appears to show a vase, but looked at once again, turns into two people, face to face. The vase resembles well-defined and precisely structured process—easy to understand though hard to change. The faces reflect practice—always unfolding in unpredictable ways, full of promise and problems, just like a conversation. The manager's challenge is to keep both images in view simultaneously.

So, to come back to where we began, the swing from business process reengineering to knowledge management did represent a radical shift in focus. But the goal for managers is not to choose between the two. Rather, the goal is to find the right balance between them—one that can grow only more important as knowledge becomes the factor that distinguishes the successful companies from the failures. Indeed, as dot-com companies mature, they're starting to search for seasoned managers who can provide their inventive, explosive communities of practice with the structure of process—but who won't suffocate practice while they're at it.

Originally published in May–June 2000
Reprint R00309

What's Your Strategy for Managing Knowledge?

MORTEN T. HANSEN, NITIN NOHRIA, AND
THOMAS TIERNEY

Executive Summary

THE RISE OF THE COMPUTER and the increasing importance of intellectual assets have compelled executives to
examine the knowledge underlying their businesses and
how it is used. Because knowledge management as a
conscious practice is so young, however, executives
have lacked models to use as guides.

To help fill that gap, the authors recently studied
knowledge management practices at management consulting firms, health care providers, and computer manufacturers. They found two very different knowledge management strategies in place.

In companies that sell relatively standardized products that fill common needs, knowledge is carefully codified and stored in databases, where it can be accessed
and used—over and over again—by anyone in the organization. The authors call this the *codification strategy*. In

companies that provide highly customized solutions to unique problems, knowledge is shared mainly through person-to-person contacts; the chief purpose of computers is to help people communicate. They call this the *personalization strategy.*

A company's choice of knowledge management strategy is not arbitrary—it must be driven by the company's competitive strategy. Emphasizing the wrong approach or trying to pursue both can quickly undermine a business. The authors warn that knowledge management should not be isolated in a functional department like HR or IT. They emphasize that the benefits are greatest—to both the company and its customers—when a CEO and other general managers actively choose one of the approaches as a primary strategy.

KNOWLEDGE MANAGEMENT is nothing new. For hundreds of years, owners of family businesses have passed their commercial wisdom on to their children, master craftsmen have painstakingly taught their trades to apprentices, and workers have exchanged ideas and know-how on the job. But it wasn't until the 1990s that chief executives started talking about knowledge management. As the foundation of industrialized economies has shifted from natural resources to intellectual assets, executives have been compelled to examine the knowledge underlying their businesses and how that knowledge is used. At the same time, the rise of networked computers has made it possible to codify, store, and share certain kinds of knowledge more easily and cheaply than ever before.

Since knowledge management as a conscious practice is so young, executives have lacked successful models that they could use as guides. To help fill that gap, we have recently studied the knowledge management practices of companies in several industries. We started by looking at management consulting firms. Because knowledge is the core asset of consultancies, they were among the first businesses to pay attention to—and make heavy investments in—the management of knowledge. They were also among the first to aggressively explore the use of information technology to capture and disseminate knowledge. Their experience, which is relevant to any company that depends on smart people and the flow of ideas, provides a window onto what works and what doesn't.

Consultants, we found, do not take a uniform approach to managing knowledge. The consulting business employs two very different knowledge management strategies. In some companies, the strategy centers on the computer. Knowledge is carefully codified and stored in databases, where it can be accessed and used easily by anyone in the company. We call this the *codification strategy*. In other companies, knowledge is closely tied to the person who developed it and is shared mainly through direct person-to-person contacts. The chief purpose of computers at such companies is to help people communicate knowledge, not to store it. We call this the *personalization strategy*. A company's choice of strategy is far from arbitrary—it depends on the way the company serves its clients, the economics of its business, and the people it hires. Emphasizing the wrong strategy or trying to pursue both at the same time can, as some consulting firms have found, quickly undermine a business.

The two strategies are not unique to consulting. When we looked beyond that business and analyzed computer companies and health care providers, we found the same two strategies at work. In fact, we believe that the choice between codification and personalization is the central one facing virtually all companies in the area of knowledge management. By better understanding the two strategies and their strengths and weaknesses, chief executives will be able to make more surefooted decisions about knowledge management and their investments in it.

The codification strategy opens up the possibility of achieving scale in knowledge reuse and thus of growing the business.

Codification or Personalization?

Some large consulting companies, such as Andersen Consulting and Ernst & Young, have pursued a codification strategy. Over the last five years, they have developed elaborate ways to codify, store, and reuse knowledge. Knowledge is codified using a "people-to-documents" approach: it is extracted from the person who developed it, made independent of that person, and reused for various purposes. Ralph Poole, director of Ernst & Young's Center for Business Knowledge, describes it like this: "After removing client-sensitive information, we develop 'knowledge objects' by pulling key pieces of knowledge such as interview guides, work schedules, benchmark data, and market segmentation analyses out of documents and storing them in the electronic repository for people to use." This approach allows many people to search for and retrieve codified knowledge without having to contact the person who originally developed it. That opens up the possibility of achieving scale in knowledge reuse and thus of growing the business.

Take the example of Randall Love, a partner in the Los Angeles office of Ernst & Young. Love was preparing an important bid for a large industrial manufacturer that needed help installing an enterprise resource planning system. He had already directed projects for implementing information systems for several manufacturers in other industries, but he hadn't yet worked on a manufacturing project in this one. He knew other Ernst & Young teams had, however, so he searched the electronic knowledge management repository for relevant knowledge. For help with the sales process, he found and used several presentations on the industry—documents containing previously developed solutions—as well as value propositions that helped him estimate how much money the client would save by implementing the system.

Because Love reused this material, Ernst & Young won the project and closed the sale in two months instead of the typical four to six. In addition, his team found programming documents, technical specifications, training materials, and change management documentation in the repository. Because these documents were available, Love and his team did not have to spend any time tracking down and talking with the people who had first developed them. The codification of such knowledge saved the team and the client one full year of work.

Ernst & Young executives have invested a lot to make sure that the codification process works efficiently. The 250 people at the Center for Business Knowledge manage the electronic repository and help consultants find and use information. Specialists write reports and analyses that many teams can use. And each of Ernst & Young's more than 40 practice areas has a staff member who helps codify and store documents. The resulting area databases are linked through a network.

Naturally, people-to-documents is not the only way consultants in firms like Ernst & Young and Andersen Consulting share knowledge—they talk with one another, of course. What is striking, however, is the degree of emphasis they place on the codification strategy.

By contrast, strategy consulting firms such as Bain, Boston Consulting Group, and McKinsey emphasize a personalization strategy. They focus on dialogue between individuals, not knowledge objects in a database. Knowledge that has not been codified—and probably couldn't be—is transferred in brainstorming sessions and one-on-one conversations. Consultants collectively arrive at deeper insights by going back and forth on problems they need to solve.

Marcia Blenko, for example, a partner in Bain's London office, had to consider a difficult strategy problem for a large British financial institution. The client wanted Bain to help it expand by offering new products and services. The assignment required geographic and product-line expertise, a broad understanding of the industry, and a large dose of creative thinking. Blenko, who had been with Bain for 12 years, knew several partners with expertise relevant to this particular problem. She left voice mail messages with them and checked Bain's "people finder" database for more contacts. Eventually she connected with nine partners and several managers who had developed growth strategies for financial services institutions. She met with a group of them in Europe, had videoconferences with others from Singapore and Sydney, and made a quick trip to Boston to attend a meeting of the financial services practice. A few of these colleagues became ongoing advisers to the project, and one of the Asian managers was assigned full time to the case team. During the next four months, Blenko and her team consulted with expert partners regularly in meetings and through phone calls and e-mail. In the process of developing a unique growth strategy, the team tapped into a worldwide network of colleagues' experience.

To make their personalization strategies work, firms like Bain invest heavily in building networks of people. Knowledge is shared not only face-to-face but also over the telephone, by e-mail, and via videoconferences.

A company's strategy for knowledge management should reflect its competitive strategy.

McKinsey fosters networks in many ways: by transferring people between offices; by supporting a culture in which consultants are expected to return phone calls from colleagues promptly; by creating directories of experts; and by using "consulting directors" within the firm to assist project teams.

These firms have also developed electronic document systems, but the purpose of the systems is not to provide knowledge objects. Instead, consultants scan documents to get up to speed in a particular area and to find out who has done work on a topic. They then approach those people directly.

When we initially looked at how consulting companies manage knowledge, we found that they all used both the codification and the personalization approaches. When we dug deeper, however, we found that effective firms excelled by focusing on one of the strategies and using the other in a supporting role. (See the table "How Consulting Firms Manage Their Knowledge.") They did not try to use both approaches to an equal degree.

How Consulting Firms Manage Their Knowledge

	Codification	Personalization
Competitive strategy	Provide high-quality, reliable, and fast information-systems implementation by reusing codified knowledge.	Provide creative, analytically rigorous advice on high-level strategic problems by channeling individual expertise.
Economic model	**Reuse Economics:** Invest once in a knowledge asset; reuse it many times. Use large teams with a high ratio of associates to partners. Focus on generating large overall revenues.	**Expert Economics:** Charge high fees for highly customized solutions to unique problems. Use small teams with a low ratio of associates to partners. Focus on maintaining high profit margins.
Knowledge management strategy	**People-to-documents:** Develop an electronic document system that codifies, stores, disseminates, and allows reuse of knowledge.	**Person-to-Person:** Develop networks for linking people so that tacit knowledge can be shared.
Information technology	Invest heavily in IT; the goal is to connect people with reusable codified knowledge.	Invest moderately in IT; the goal is to facilitate conversations and the exchange of tacit knowledge.
Human resources	Hire new college graduates who are well suited to the reuse of knowledge and the implementation of solutions. Train people in groups and through computer-based distance learning. Reward people for using and contributing to document databases.	Hire M.B.A.s who like problem solving and can tolerate ambiguity. Train people through one-on-one mentoring. Reward people for directly sharing knowledge with others.
Examples	Andersen Consulting, Ernst & Young	McKinsey & Company, Bain & Company

Different Strategies, Different Drivers

A company's knowledge management strategy should reflect its competitive strategy: how it creates value for customers, how that value supports an economic model, and how the company's people deliver on the value and the economics.

CREATING VALUE FOR CUSTOMERS

Randall Love's approach to implementing the information system is typical of consulting companies where the efficient reuse of codified knowledge is essential because they are dealing with similar problems over and over. In such firms, the service offering is very clear: the customer benefits because the consultants can build a reliable, high-quality information system faster and at a better price than others by using work plans, software code, and solutions that have been fine-tuned and proven successful. That's not to say that the process operates on automatic pilot. It's like building with Lego blocks: consultants reuse existing bricks while applying their skills to construct something new.

Strategy consulting firms offer customers a very different kind of value. Consultants like Marcia Blenko tackle problems that don't have clear solutions at the outset. They seek advice from colleagues to deepen their understanding of the issues, but in the end they must create a highly customized solution to a unique problem. Because their clients' problems are difficult and one of a kind, the consultants can charge high fees for their services.

TURNING A PROFIT

Companies that follow a codification strategy rely on the "economics of reuse." Once a knowledge asset—software code or a manual, for example—is developed and paid for, it can be used many times over at very low cost, provided it does not have to be substantially modified each time it is used. Because the knowledge is contained in electronic repositories, it can be employed in many jobs by many consultants. Many consultants can be assigned to a project; big projects will have a high ratio of consultants to partners. For example, there are more than 30 consultants for each partner at Andersen Consulting.

The reuse of knowledge saves work, reduces communications costs, and allows a company to take on more projects. As a consequence, firms such as Andersen Consulting and Ernst & Young have been able to grow at rates of 20% or more in recent years. Ernst & Young's worldwide consulting revenues, for example, increased from $1.5 billion in 1995 to $2.7 billion in 1997.

By contrast, the personalization strategy relies on the logic of "expert economics." Strategy consulting firms offer their clients advice that is rich in tacit knowledge. The process of sharing deep knowledge is time consuming, expensive, and slow. It can't truly be systematized, so it can't be made efficient. That means, first, that the ratio of consultants to partners in these firms is relatively low—there are approximately seven consultants for each partner at McKinsey and Bain. And second, it means that it's difficult to hire many new consultants in a short period because every new person needs so much one-on-one training. For those two reasons, strategy consulting firms find it difficult to grow rapidly without sacrificing the customized approach.

Nevertheless, their highly customized offerings allow them to charge much higher prices than firms offering more standardized services can. In 1997, for example, daily fees for a McKinsey consultant were on average more than $2,000; at Andersen Consulting, the figure was slightly more than $600.

MANAGING PEOPLE

Not surprisingly, the two kinds of firms hire different kinds of people and train and reward them differently. Ernst & Young and Andersen Consulting hire undergraduates from top universities and train them to develop and implement change programs and information systems. Andersen's recruits are trained at the firm's Center for Professional Education, a 150-acre campus in St. Charles, Illinois. Using the knowledge management repository, the consultants work through scenarios designed to improve business processes. They are implementers, not inventors; the "not invented here" attitude has no place in a reuse firm.

McKinsey, BCG, and Bain hire top-tier M.B.A. graduates to be inventors—that is, to use their analytic and creative skills on unique business problems. These firms also want people who will be able to use the person-to-person knowledge-sharing approach effectively. To be sure of obtaining people with that mix of skills, they recruit with extraordinary care. Partners and senior consultants interview a candidate six to eight times before making a job offer. At Bain, 1 out of 60 applicants gets an offer. Once on board, their most important training comes from working with experienced consultants who act as mentors.

From Health Care to High Tech

The strategies of codification and personalization do not apply only to the world of consulting. We found that providers of health care and manufacturers of computers also need to choose a knowledge management approach that fits their needs and goals.

Access Health, a call-in medical center, exploits a reuse model. When someone calls the center, a registered nurse uses the company's "clinical decision architecture" to assess the caller's symptoms, rule out possible conditions, and recommend a home remedy, doctor's visit, or emergency room trip. The knowledge repository contains algorithms of the symptoms of more than 500 illnesses. CEO Joseph Tallman describes the company's strategy: "We are not inventing a new way to cure disease. We are taking available knowledge and inventing processes to put it to better use."

Access Health provides a prime example of the benefits that come from reusing codified knowledge—in this instance, software algorithms. The company spent a lot to develop those algorithms, but it has been repaid handsomely for its investment. The first 300 algorithms that Access Health developed have each been used an average of 8,000 times per year. That level of reuse allows it to charge low prices per call. In turn, the company's paying customers—insurance companies and provider groups—save money because many callers would have made expensive trips to the emergency room or doctor's office when they could have been diagnosed over the phone.

Contrast Access Health's reuse strategy with the highly developed personalization model used at Memorial Sloan-Kettering Cancer Center in New York City. The center provides the best, most customized advice and treatment to cancer patients. A variety of experts consults on each patient's case, and managing the experts' collaboration is, in essence, managing the center's knowledge. Dr. James Dougherty, its deputy physician in chief, describes this collaboration as follows: "We coordinate intensive face-to-face communication in order to ensure that knowledge is transferred between researchers and clinicians and between different types of clinicians." Employees work together in 17 disease-specific teams. The breast cancer team, for example, has 40 specialists—medical oncologists, surgeons, radiation therapists, psychologists, and others—as well as a core of basic scientists.

To make person-to-person communication easy, a team's members are all located in the same area of the hospital. Each team has several face-to-face meetings per week that everyone attends. The meetings cover basic science initiatives, clinical findings, patient care, and ongoing research.

The center's human resource policy is aligned with its knowledge management strategy. Top cancer clinicians are attracted by Memorial Sloan-Kettering's state-of-the-art technology and excellent reputation. These clinicians are highly paid—most receive salaries that place them in the ninety-fifth percentile or above relative to their counterparts at other academic institutions. The center hires clinicians from two pools of candidates. Junior people are hired from top university residency programs and trained as fellows. The best fellows are moved into an "up or out" pyramid system. The center also hires senior, nationally recognized clinicians who often bring teams of people with them.

It is hard to imagine two business models in the same industry as different as those of Access Health and Memorial Sloan-Kettering. Yet both assess patients' symptoms and make recommendations for their care, and both are highly successful. By providing reliable service at low cost, Access Health has captured 50% of the call-center market and is growing at 40% a year. One insurer using its services saw its emergency-room admissions drop by 15% and its physician office visits by 11%. For its part, Memorial Sloan-Kettering is consistently ranked as the top cancer research and treatment institution in the country.

Medicine, like management consulting and other services, is built on unique knowledge. But the two knowledge management models also apply in the industrial sector. Consider the very different approaches taken by two computer companies, Dell and Hewlett-Packard.

Dell's competitive strategy is to assemble inexpensive PCs that are made to order and sell them directly to customers. A sophisticated knowledge management system lies behind that business model. Dell has invested heavily in an electronic repository that contains a list of available components. The system drives the operation: customers choose configurations from a menu, suppliers provide components based on their orders, and manufacturing retrieves orders from the system and schedules assembly. Dell does not deliver highly customized orders, and it raises its prices considerably for orders with special components.

Dell has to invest a good deal up front to determine and specify configurations, but its investment pays off because of the knowledge's reuse. In 1997, Dell shipped 11 million PCs. Those systems were put together from 40,000 possible configurations (competitors typically offer only about 100 configurations), which means that each configuration was used on average 275 times. That level of reuse allows Dell to lower its costs and charge less than the competition. Propelled in part by its knowledge reuse model, Dell's net income for 1997 was $944 million on sales of $12.3 billion; the company's revenues have grown 83% annually over the last four years.

Hewlett-Packard, by contrast, uses a personalization approach to support its business strategy, which is to develop innovative products. For that strategy to succeed, technical knowledge must get transferred to product development teams in a timely way. The company channels such knowledge through person-to-person exchanges.

For example, engineers routinely use one of the company's planes to visit other divisions and share ideas about possible new products. Rather than limiting travel budgets, executives encourage such travel. Every employee has access to the corporate airplanes, which travel daily between HP offices. Remarkably, the company manages effective person-to-person knowledge sharing despite its size—with 120,000 employees, HP dwarfs the largest consulting company, Andersen Consulting, which has about 60,000 people.

Consider this example. An HP team recently developed a very successful electronic oscilloscope with a Windows operating system and interface. Executives wanted to be sure that other divisions understood and applied the interface. To keep the costs of knowledge transfer low, they considered trying to codify the acquired know-how. They realized, however, that the knowledge they wanted to capture was too rich and subtle to incorporate in a written report. And they understood that writing answers to the many questions that would come from HP's divisions would take an extraordinary amount of time. So they took the person-to-person approach and sent engineers from product development teams to meetings at divisions around the world and to a companywide conference.

The executives' decision didn't come cheap: by one estimate, the company spent $1 million on communication costs alone on this process. But the investment paid off as the interface gained widespread acceptance throughout the company.

In all the companies and institutions we examined, managers had chosen a distinct knowledge management strategy. Although their approaches differed slightly, there was a common pattern among them. Those that pursued an assemble-to-order product or service strategy emphasized the codification and reuse of knowledge. Those that pursued highly customized service offerings, or a product innovation strategy, invested mainly in person-to-person knowledge sharing.

The strategy consulting firms we studied all came to grief with document-driven systems.

Do Not Straddle

As we've said, companies that use knowledge effectively pursue one strategy predominantly and use the second strategy to support the first. We think of this as an 80–20 split: 80% of their knowledge sharing follows one strategy, 20% the other. Executives who try to excel at both strategies risk failing at both. Management consulting firms have run into serious trouble when they failed to stick with one approach.

The strategy consulting firms we studied all came to grief with document-driven systems. Consultants were tempted to use the systems to deliver standardized solutions, but their customers were paying for highly customized services. When the systems were misused, customers became dissatisfied.

As the CEO of a major U.S. company told us, "I have been using a particular consulting company for over a decade now. One of the main reasons I have used them so regularly is because they have intimate knowledge of my company and our industry. The firm's partners who have worked with me also know my style and my strengths and weaknesses. The advice I have gotten from them has been sensitive to our unique needs. Recently, though, I have found that they are trying to push cookie-cutter solutions. It's almost as if they are simply changing the names on the same set of presentations. While some of their advice is useful, I am not sure if that's enough. Frankly I expect more—and they sure as hell have not reduced their rates."

Another consulting firm, Bain, learned a hard lesson about relying on documents. In the 1980s, before electronic document systems became fashionable, managers at Bain developed a large paper-based document center at its Boston headquarters; it stored slide books containing disguised presentations, analyses, and information on various industries. The library's purpose was to help consultants learn from work done in the past without having to contact the teams that did the work. But as one partner commented, "The center offered a picture of a cake without giving out the recipe." The documents could not convey the richness of the knowledge or the logic that had been applied to reach solutions—that understanding had to be communicated from one person to another. Bain's management eventually developed an entirely new system, but the failed approach wasted time and money.

Other strategy consulting companies report different problems with electronic document systems. For example, after subject experts at one firm contributed documents to electronic libraries, they were flooded with callers asking very basic questions. Two companies that we studied have scrapped their investment in electronic knowledge databases; their existing databases are used simply to connect people.

Similarly, firms that rely on codification have run into trouble by overinvesting in person-to-person systems. When they overinvest in this way, they undermine their value proposition—reliable systems at reasonable prices—as well as the economics of reuse. That's because their people may feel encouraged to develop a novel solution to a problem even when a perfectly good solution already exists in the electronic repository. Unnecessary innovations are expensive: programming and then debugging new software, for instance, eats a lot of resources. And person-to-person knowledge sharing involves expensive travel and meeting time; those costs dilute the advantage that is created when codified knowledge is reused. (See "Getting the Incentives Right" at the end of this article.)

Companies that straddle the two strategies may also find themselves with an unwieldy mix of people. Having both inventors and implementers rubbing elbows can be deadly. The downfall of CSC Index, the consulting company that invented the reengineering concept in the early 1990s, underscores how serious this problem can be.

The founders of what was originally known simply as Index had strong backgrounds in IT systems. Success with reengineering, however, catapulted the company into the general management arena. It then tried to leverage its newfound access to the CEO by aggressively hiring senior consultants from established strategy consulting firms. It also started to recruit M.B.A.s from leading business schools. Soon the firm had two populations: an old guard that focused on IT systems and had strong implementation skills, and a new guard that focused on corporate strategy and had strong conceptual skills.

As reengineering became a commodity business later in the decade, some of the old guard recognized the need to standardize their methods and create more reusable knowledge. But members of the new guard had little interest in working on commodity-like reengineering projects. They had joined the firm because they wanted to work on cutting-edge strategy problems.

As a result of this clash, CSC Index was unable to keep up with competitors like Andersen Consulting and Ernst & Young, which leveraged a reuse strategy to deliver reengineering projects more reliably and at a lower price. Nor did the firm have enough depth in strategy consulting to compete with the likes of McKinsey, BCG, and Bain. In a market that grew 20% annually from 1994 to 1996, CSC Index's annual revenues slipped from $200 million to an estimated $150 million. The firm was subsequently folded into its parent company. (See "How Much Information Technology Do You Need?" at the end of this article.)

Although it is important to avoid straddling, an exclusive focus on one strategy is also unwise. Companies pursuing the personalization model should have a modest electronic document system that supports people in two ways: by providing background materials on a topic and by pointing them to experts who can provide further advice. As Mark Horwitch, a partner at Bain, explains, "Information in firms pursuing the person-to-person approach is leveraged as an input to the analytical process rather than as an output."

Companies that primarily adhere to the reuse model will want about 20% of their knowledge sharing to be person-to-person. Thus they will have to pay to bring some people within the company together at meetings. They should encourage the heavy use of e-mail and electronic discussion forums. Such person-to-person communication is needed to make sure that documents are not blindly applied to situations for which they are ill suited.

Choosing the Right Strategy

Competitive strategy must drive knowledge management strategy. Executives must be able to articulate why customers buy a company's products or services rather than those of its competitors. What value do customers expect from the company? How does knowledge that resides in the company add value for customers? If a company does not have clear answers to those questions, it should not attempt to choose a knowledge management strategy because it could easily make a bad choice.

Assuming the competitive strategy is clear, managers will want to consider three further questions that can help them choose a primary knowledge management strategy. Although the implications of the answers may seem obvious, it is important for managers to make the explicit connection between their company's competitive strategy and how they use knowledge to support it.

Do you offer standardized or customized products?
Companies that follow a standardized product strategy sell products that do not vary much, if at all. Even Dell,

whose assemble-to-order computers vary more than mass-marketed products, sells products that can be considered standardized. A knowledge management strategy based on reuse fits companies that are creating standardized products.

A company sells customized products and services if most of its work goes toward meeting particular customers' unique needs. Because those needs will vary dramatically, codified knowledge is of limited value. Companies that follow a customized product approach should consider the personalization model.

Do you have a mature or innovative product? A business strategy based on mature products typically benefits most from a reuse model. The processes for developing and selling such products involve well-understood tasks and knowledge that can be codified. A strategy based on product innovation, on the other hand, is best supported by a personalization strategy. People in companies seeking innovation need to share information that would get lost in document form.

Do your people rely on explicit or tacit knowledge to solve problems? Explicit knowledge is knowledge that can be codified, such as simple software code and market data. When a company's employees rely on explicit knowledge to do their work, the people-to-documents approach makes the most sense. Tacit knowledge, by contrast, is difficult to articulate in writing and is acquired through personal experience. It includes scientific expertise, operational know-how, insights about an industry, business judgment, and technological expertise. When people use tacit knowledge most often to solve problems, the person-to-person approach works best.

Managers sometimes try to turn inherently tacit knowledge into explicit knowledge. That can lead to serious problems. Xerox, for example, once attempted to embed the know-how of its service and repair technicians into an expert system that was installed in the copiers. They hoped that technicians responding to a call could be guided by the system and complete repairs from a distance. But it turned out that technicians could not solve problems using the system by itself. When the copier designers looked into the matter more closely, they discovered that technicians learned from one another by sharing stories about how they had fixed the machines. The expert system could not replicate the nuance and detail that were exchanged in face-to-face conversations.

Your answers to the three questions above will often suggest which knowledge management strategy to emphasize. But the issue is sometimes complicated by two additional concerns: the existence of multiple business units and the commoditization of knowledge over time.

It is tempting to think that the two knowledge management models can coexist in different business units within one corporation. Indeed, they can coexist—but only in corporations where business units operate like stand-alone companies. In a company like General Motors, where the car divisions have little to do with the credit and finance divisions, different models can in fact work in each business unit. Companies with tightly integrated business units, however, should either focus on only one of the strategies or spin off units that don't fit the mold.

Some knowledge-intensive products and services— like reengineering consulting, for example—mature over time and become commodities. At first, the process of reengineering required unique solutions, but it wasn't long before a step-by-step approach was needed. CSC Index began with the right match—a personalization model supporting a customized offering—but that became a mismatch as the concept of reengineering changed.

Companies that isolate knowledge management in functional departments like HR or IT risk losing its benefits.

The firm had a choice: change its knowledge management strategy or get out of the reengineering business. By not choosing either, it fell on difficult times.

In effective companies, the knowledge management model stays the same even as new products and services mature. For consulting companies focused on highly customized solutions, the trick is to get out of areas like reengineering before they become commodities. At firms that reuse knowledge and solutions, the opposite is true: such firms exploit an approach as it matures. Peter Novins, a partner at Ernst & Young, puts it like this: "We try to commoditize the expertise in one area as fast as possible and move it to scale and reuse, which benefits both the client and the company."

Don't Isolate Knowledge Management

Some CEOs have put knowledge management at the top of their agendas. Others have not given it the same attention as they have given cost cutting, restructuring, or international expansion. In companies where that is the case, knowledge management takes place—if at all—in functional departments such as HR or IT. But companies that isolate knowledge management risk losing its benefits, which are highest when it is coordinated with HR, IT, and competitive strategy.

That coordination requires the leadership of the general manager. When CEOs and general managers actively choose a knowledge management approach—one that supports a clear competitive strategy—both the company and its customers benefit. When top people fail to make such a choice, both suffer. Customers may end up paying for a customized solution when a standard solution would have worked perfectly well. Or they may get paint-by-the-numbers advice when they really need help with a unique problem. Within the organization, employees will be confused about priorities. The issue will quickly become politicized, and people will battle for resources without seeing the whole picture. Only strong leadership can provide the direction a company needs to choose, implement, and overcome resistance to a new knowledge management strategy.

Getting the Incentives Right

PEOPLE NEED INCENTIVES to participate in the knowledge sharing process. The two knowledge management strategies call for different incentive systems. In the codification model, managers need to develop a system that encourages people to write down what they know and to get those documents into the electronic repository. And real incentives—not small enticements—are required to get people to take those steps. In fact, the level and quality of employees' contributions to the document database should be part of their annual performance reviews. Ernst & Young, for example, does just that. At performance reviews, consultants are evaluated along five dimensions, one of which is their "contribution to and utilization of the knowledge asset of the firm."

Incentives to stimulate knowledge sharing should be very different at companies that are following the personalization approach. Managers need to reward people for sharing knowledge directly with other people. At Bain, the partners are evaluated each year on a variety of dimensions, including how much direct help they have given colleagues. The degree of high-quality person-to-person dialogue a partner has had with others can account for as much as one-quarter of his or her annual compensation.

How Much Information Technology Do You Need?

THE LEVEL OF IT support a company needs depends on its choice of knowledge management strategy. For the codification model, heavy IT support is critical; for the personalization model, it is much less important. Managers who are implementing the former should be prepared to spend a lot on large, sophisticated electronic repository systems. Andersen Consulting, for example, has developed proprietary search engines. Ernst & Young has installed a hierarchy of databases. At the top are "elite" databases that are restricted in size and contain the best knowledge on a particular topic. Next come larger databases containing specific "knowledge objects"; finally there are the much larger "holding tanks" for all kinds of other materials.

Over the past few years, Andersen Consulting and

Ernst & Young have each spent more than $500 million on IT and people to support their knowledge management strategies. On a much smaller scale, Access Health initially invested $16 million in its knowledge management system when its revenues were a modest $20 million; later it spent another $40 million on the system in order to have sufficient scale to generate $100 million in revenues.

The two knowledge management strategies require different IT infrastructures as well as different levels of support. In the codification model, managers need to implement a system that is much like a traditional library—it must contain a large cache of documents and include search engines that allow people to find and use the documents they need. In the personalization model, it's most important to have a system that allows people to find other people.

Originally published in March–April 1999
Reprint 99206

Good Communication That Blocks Learning

CHRIS ARGYRIS

Executive Summary

THE NEW BUT NOW FAMILIAR TECHNIQUES of corporate communication—focus groups, surveys, management-by-walking-around—can block organizational learning even as they help solve certain kinds of problems. These techniques do help gather simple, single-loop information. But they also promote defensive reasoning by encouraging employees to believe that their proper role is to criticize management while the proper role of management is to take action and fix whatever is wrong.

Worse yet, they discourage double-loop learning, which is the process of asking questions not only about objective facts but also about the reasons and motives behind those facts. Double-loop learning encourages people to examine their own behavior, take personal responsibility for their own action and inaction, and surface the kind of potentially threatening or embarrassing information that can produce real change.

The problem is not that employees run away from this kind of organizational self-examination, the problem is that no one asks it of them. Managers focus so earnestly on "positive" values—employee satisfaction, upbeat attitude, high morale—that it wold strike them as destructive to make demands on employee self-awareness. Yet employees dig deeper and harder into the truth when the task of scrutinizing the organization includes looking at their own roles, responsibilities, and potential contributions to corrective action.

The criteria for effectiveness have risen sharply in recent years. Today managers need employees who think constantly and creatively about the needs of the organization, employees with as much intrinsic motivation and as deep a sense of organizational stewardship as any company executive.

Twenty-first-century corporations will find it hard to survive, let alone flourish, unless they get better work from their employees. This does not necessarily mean harder work or more work. What it does necessarily mean is employees who've learned to take active responsibility for their own behavior, develop and share first-rate information about their jobs, and make good use of genuine empowerment to shape lasting solutions to fundamental problems.

This is not news. Most executives understand that tougher competition will require more effective learning, broader empowerment, and greater commitment from everyone in the company. Moreover, they understand that the key to better performance is better communication. For 20 years or more, business leaders have used a score of communication tools—focus groups, organizational surveys, management-by-walking-around, and others—to convey and to gather the information needed to bring about change.

What *is* news is that these familiar techniques, used correctly, will actually inhibit the learning and communication that twenty-first-century corporations will require not just of managers but of every employee. For years, I have watched corporate leaders talking to subordinates at every level in order to find out what actually goes on in their companies and then help it go on more effectively. What I have observed is that the methods these executives use to tackle relatively simple problems actually prevent them from getting the kind of deep information, insightful behavior, and productive change they need to cope with the much more complex problem of organizational renewal.

Years ago, when corporations still wanted employees who did only what they were told, employee surveys and walk-around management were appropriate and effective tools. They can still produce useful information about routine issues like cafeteria service and parking privileges, and they can still generate valuable quantitative data in support of programs like total quality management. What they do *not* do is get people to reflect on their work and behavior. They do not encourage individual accountability. And they do not surface the kinds of deep and potentially threatening or embarrassing information that can motivate learning and produce real change.

Let me give an example of what I mean. Not long ago, I worked with a company conducting a TQM initiative. TQM has been highly successful at cutting unnecessary costs, so successful that many companies have raised it to the status of a management philosophy. In this particular case, a TQM consultant worked with top management to carry out a variety of surveys and group meetings to help 40 supervisors identify nine areas in which they could tighten procedures and reduce costs. The resulting initiative met its goals one month early and saved more money than management had anticipated. The CEO was so elated that he treated the entire team to a champagne dinner to celebrate what was clearly a victory for everyone involved.

I had regular conversations with the supervisors throughout the implementation, and I was struck by two often-repeated comments. First, the supervisors told me several times how easy it had been to identify the nine target areas since they knew in advance where the worst inefficiencies might be found. Second, they complained again and again that fixing the nine areas was long overdue, that it was high time management took action. As one supervisor put it, "Thank God for TQM!"

I asked several supervisors how long they had known about the nine problem areas, and their responses ranged from three to five years. I then asked them why, if they'd known about the problems, they'd never taken action themselves. "Why 'Thank God for TQM'?" I said. "Why not 'Thank God for the supervisors'?"

None of the supervisors hesitated to answer these questions. They cited the blindness and timidity of management. They blamed interdepartmental competitiveness verging on warfare. They said the culture of the company made it unacceptable to get others into trouble for the sake of correcting problems. In every explanation, the responsibility for fixing the nine problem areas belonged to someone else. The supervisors were loyal, honest managers. The blame lay elsewhere.

What was really going on in this company? To begin with, we can identify two different problems. Cost reduction is one. The other is a group of employees who stand passively by and watch inefficiencies develop and persevere. TQM produces the simple learning necessary to effect a solution to the first problem. But TQM will not prevent a recurrence of the second problem or cause the supervisors to wonder why they never acted. To understand why this is so, we need to know more about how learning takes place and about at least two mechanisms that keep it from taking place at all.

As I have emphasized in my previous articles on learning in the workplace, learning occurs in two forms: single-loop and double-loop. Single-loop learning asks a one-dimensional question to elicit a one-dimensional answer. My favorite example is a thermostat, which measures ambient temperature against a standard setting and turns the heat source on or off accordingly. The whole transaction is binary.

Double-loop learning takes an additional step or, more often than not, several additional steps. It turns the question back on the questioner. It asks what the media call follow-ups. In the case of the thermostat, for instance, double-loop learning would wonder whether the current setting was actually the most effective temperature at which to keep the room and, if so, whether the present heat source was the most effective means of achieving it. A double-loop process might also ask why the current setting was chosen in the first place. In other words, double-loop learning asks questions not only about objective facts but also about the reasons and motives behind those facts.

Here is a simple illustration of the difference between these two kinds of learning: A CEO who had begun to practice his own form of management-by-walking-around learned from his employees that the company inhibited innovation by subjecting every new idea to more than 275 separate checks and sign-offs. He promptly appointed a task force to look at this situation, and it eliminated 200 of the obstacles. The result was a higher innovation rate.

This may sound like a successful managerial intervention. The CEO discovers a counterproductive process and, with the cooperation of others, produces dramatic improvement. Yet I would call it a case of single-loop learning. It addresses a difficulty but ignores a more fundamental problem. A more complete diagnosis—that is to say, a double-loop approach to this situation—would require the CEO to ask the employees who told him about the sign-offs some tougher questions about company culture and their own behavior. For example, "How long have you known about the 275 required sign-offs?" Or "What goes on in this company that prevented you from questioning these practices and getting them corrected or eliminated?"

Why didn't the CEO ask these questions of the supervisor? And why didn't the 40 supervisors ask these questions of themselves? There are two closely related mechanisms at work here—one social, the other psychological.

The social reason that the CEO did not dig deeper is that doing so might have been seen as putting people on the spot. Unavoidably, digging deeper would have uncovered the employees' collusion with the inefficient process. Their motives were probably quite decent—they didn't want to open Pandora's box, didn't want to be negative. But their behavior—and the behavior of the CEO in ignoring this dimension of the problem—combined with everyone's failure to examine his or her indi-

vidual behavior and blocked the kind of learning that is
crucial to organizational effectiveness.

In the name of positive thinking, in other words, managers often censor what everyone needs to say and hear.
For the sake of "morale" and "considerateness," they
deprive employees and themselves of the opportunity to
take responsibility for their own behavior by learning to
understand it. Because double-loop learning depends on
questioning one's own assumptions and behavior, this
apparently benevolent strategy is actually *anti*learning.
Admittedly, being considerate and positive can contribute to the solution of single-loop problems like cutting costs. But it will never help people figure out why
they lived with problems for years on end, why they covered up those problems, why they covered up the cover-
up, why they were so good at pointing to the responsibility of others and so slow to focus on their own. The 40
supervisors said it was high time that management took
steps. None of them asked why they themselves had
never even drawn management's attention to nine areas
of waste and inefficiency.

What we see here is managers using socially "up-beat"
behavior to inhibit learning. What we do not see, at least
not readily, is why anyone should want to inhibit learning. The reason lies in a set of deeper and more complex
psychological motives.

Consider again the story of the 40 supervisors. TQM's
rigorous, linear reasoning solves a set of important, single-loop problems. But while we see some effective single-loop learning, no double-loop learning occurs at all.
Instead, the moment the important problems involve
potential threat or embarrassment, rigorous reasoning
goes right out the window and *defensive reasoning* takes
over. Note how the supervisors deftly sidestep all respon-

sibility and defend themselves against the charge of inaction—or worse, collusion—by blaming others. In fact, what I call defensive reasoning serves no purpose except self-protection, though the people who use it rarely acknowledge that they are protecting themselves. It is the group, the department, the organization that they are protecting, in the name of being positive. They believe themselves to be using the kind of rigorous thinking employed in TQM, which identifies problems, gathers objective data, postulates causes, tests explanations, and derives corrective action, all along relatively scientific lines. But the supervisors' actual techniques—gathering data selectively, postulating only causes that do not threaten themselves, testing explanations in ways that are sloppy and self-serving—are a parody of scientific method. The supervisors are not protecting others; they are blaming them. They have learned this procedure carefully over time, supported at each step by defensive organizational rationalizations like "caring" and "thoughtfulness."

The reason the supervisors fail to question their own rather remarkable behavior—the reason they so instinctively and thoroughly avoid double-loop learning—is psychological. It has to do with the mental models that we all develop early in life for dealing with emotional or threatening issues.

In the process of growing up, all of us learn and warehouse master programs for dealing with difficult situations. These programs are sets of rules we use to design our own actions and interpret the actions of others. We retrieve them whenever we need to diagnose a problem or invent or size up a solution. Without them, we'd have to start from scratch each time we faced a challenge.

One of the puzzling things about these mental models

is that when the issues we face are embarrassing or threatening, the master programs we actually use are rarely the ones we think we use. Each of us has what I call an *espoused theory of action* based on principles and precepts that fit our intellectual backgrounds and commitments. But most of us have quite a different *theory-in-use* to which we resort in moments of stress. And very few of us are aware of the contradiction between the two. In short, most of us are consistently inconsistent in the way we act.

Espoused theories differ widely, but most theories-in-use have the same set of four governing values. All of us design our behavior in order to remain in unilateral control, to maximize winning and minimize losing, to suppress negative feelings, and to be as rational as possible, by which we mean laying out clear-cut goals and then evaluating our own behavior on the basis of whether or not we've achieved them.

The purpose of this strategy is to avoid vulnerability, risk, embarrassment, and the appearance of incompetence. In other words, it is a deeply defensive strategy and a recipe for ineffective learning. We might even call it a recipe for antilearning, because it helps us avoid reflecting on the counterproductive consequences of our own behavior. Theories-in-use assume a world that prizes unilateral control and winning above all else, and in that world, we focus primarily on controlling others and on making sure that we are not ourselves controlled. If any reflection does occur, it is in the service of winning and controlling, not of opening ourselves to learning.

Defensive strategies discourage reflection in another way as well. Because we practice them most of our lives, we are all highly skilled at carrying them out. Skilled actions are second nature; we rarely reflect on what we take for granted.

In studies of more than 6,000 people, I have found this kind of defensive theory-in-use to be universal, with no measurable difference by country, age, sex, ethnic identity, education, wealth, power, or experience. All over the world, in every kind of business and organization, in every kind of crisis and dilemma, the principles of defensive reasoning encourage people to leave their own behavior unexamined and to avoid any objective test of their premises and conclusions.

As if this individual defensive reasoning were not enough of a problem, genuine learning in organizations is inhibited by a second universal phenomenon that I call *organizational defensive routines.* These consist of all the policies, practices, and actions that prevent human beings from having to experience embarrassment or threat and, at the same time, prevent them from examining the nature and causes of that embarrassment or threat.

Take face-saving. To work, it must be unacknowledged. If you tell your subordinate Fred that you are saving his face, you have defeated your own purpose. What you do tell Fred is a fiction about the success of his own decision and a lie about your reasons for rescinding it. What's more, if Fred correctly senses the mixed message, he will almost certainly say nothing.

The logic here, as in all organizational defensive routines, is unmistakable: send a mixed message ("Your decision was a good one, and I'm overruling it"); pretend it is not mixed ("You can be proud of your contribution"); make the mixed message and the pretense undiscussable ("I feel good about this outcome, and I'm sure you do too"); and, finally, make the undiscussability undiscussable ("Now that I've explained everything to your satisfaction, is there anything *else* you'd like to talk about?").

Defensive reasoning occurs when individuals make their premises and inferences tacit, then draw conclusions that cannot be tested except by the tenets of this tacit logic. Nothing could be more detrimental to organizational learning than this process of elevating individual defensive tactics to an organizational routine.

Yet whenever managers are trying to get at the truth about problems that are embarrassing or threatening, they are likely to stumble into the same set of predictable pitfalls. Asked to examine their own behavior or the behavior of subordinates, people in this situation are likely:

- To reason defensively and to interact with others who are reasoning defensively;

- To get superficial, single-loop responses that lead to superficial, single-loop solutions;

- To reinforce the organizational defensive routines that inhibit access to valid information and genuine learning;

- To be unaware of their own defenses because these are so skilled and automatic; and

- To be unaware that they are producing any of these consequences, or, if they *are* aware of defensiveness, to see it only in others.

Given all these built-in barriers to self-understanding and self-examination under threatening conditions, it is a wonder that organizational learning takes place at all. It is an even greater wonder when we realize that many of the forms of communication that management works so hard to perfect actually reinforce those barriers. Yet this is exactly what they do.

We have seen a couple of examples of management's "benevolent" censorship of true but negative messages. In addition, we have looked at the psychological mechanisms that lead employees, supervisors, managers, and executives to engage in personal and collective defensive routines. The question we still have to answer is precisely how modern corporate communications succeed in actually contributing to this censorship and these defensive routines.

They do so in two explicit ways. First, they create a bias against personal learning and commitment in the way they parcel out roles and responsibilities in every survey, dialogue, and conversation. Second, they open a door to defensive reasoning—and close one on individual self-awareness—in the way they continuously emphasize extrinsic as opposed to intrinsic motivation.

First, consider the way roles and responsibilities are assigned in manager-employee (or leader-subordinate) conversations, interviews, and surveys. There seem to be two rules. Rule number one is that employees are to be truthful and forthcoming about the world they work in, about norms, procedures, and the strengths and weaknesses of their superiors. All other aspects of their role in the life of the organization—their goals, feelings, failings, and conflicted motives—are taken for granted and remain unexamined. Rule number two is that top-level managers, who play an intensely scrutinized role in the life of the company, are to assume virtually all responsibility for employee well-being and organizational success. Employees must tell the truth as they see it; leaders must modify their own and the company's behavior. In other words, employees educate, and managers act.

Take the case of Acme, a large, multinational energy company with 6,000 employees. Under increasing competitive pressure, the company was forced to downsize, and to no one's surprise, morale was failing fast. To learn as much as possible about its own shortcomings and how to correct them, Acme management designed and conducted an employee survey with the help of experts, and 95% of employees responded. Of those responding, 75% agreed on five positive points:

- They were proud to work for Acme.

- Their job satisfaction was very high.

- They found their immediate supervisors fair and technically competent.

- They believed management was concerned for their welfare.

- They felt competent to perform their own jobs.

Some 65% of the respondents also indicated some concerns:

- They were skeptical about management's capacity to take initiative, communicate candidly, and act effectively.

- They described Acme's corporate culture as one of blame.

- They complained that managers, while espousing empowerment, were strongly attached to their own unilateral control.

The CEO read the first set of findings to mean that employees were basically satisfied and loyal. He saw the second set as a list of problems that he must make a serious effort to correct. And so the CEO replaced several top managers and arranged for the reeducation of the whole management team, including himself and his direct reports. He announced that Acme would no longer tolerate a culture of blame. He introduced training programs to make managers more forthright and better able to take initiative. And he promised to place greater emphasis on genuine empowerment.

The CEO's logic went like this: My employees will identify the problems. I'll fix them by creating a new vision, defining new practices and policies, and selecting a top management team genuinely committed to them. Change will inevitably follow.

I think most managers would call this a success story. If we dig deeper, however, we see a pattern I've observed hundreds of times. Underneath the CEO's aggressive action, important issues have been bypassed, and the bypass has been covered up.

When the CEO took his new team on a five-day retreat to develop the new strategy and plan its implementation, he invited me to come along. In the course of the workshop, I asked each participant to write a simple case in a format I have found to be a powerful tool in predicting how executives will deal with difficult issues during implementation. The method also reveals contradictions between what the executives say and what they do and highlights their awareness of these discrepancies.

I asked each member of the team to write one or two sentences describing one important barrier to the new strategy and another three or four sentences telling how they would overcome that barrier. Then I asked them to split the rest of the page in half. On one side, they were to write an actual or imagined dialogue with a subordinate about the issue in question. On the other side, they were to note any unsaid or unsayable thoughts or feelings they might have about this conversation. I asked them to continue this script for several pages. When they were finished, the group as a whole discussed each case at some length, and we recorded the discussions. The ability to replay key sections made it easier for the participants to score themselves on candor, forthrightness, and the extent to which their comments and behavior encouraged genuine employee commitment—the three values that the CEO had directed the executives to foster.

All of the executives chose genuinely important issues around resistance to change. But all of them dealt with the resistance they expected from subordinates by easing in, covering up, and avoiding candor and plain speaking. They did so in the name of minimizing subordinates' defensiveness and in hopes of getting them to buy into change. The implicit logic behind their scripts went something like this:

- Hide your fears about the other person's likely resistance to change. Cover this fear with persistent positiveness. Pretend the two of you agree, especially when you know you don't.

- Deal with resistant responses by stressing the problem rather than the resistance. Be positive. Keep this strategy a secret.

- If this approach doesn't work, make it clear that you won't take no for an answer. After all, you're the boss.

Imagine this kind of logic applied to sensitive issues in hundreds of conversations with employees. It's not hard to guess what the response will be, and it certainly isn't buy-in.

What happened to candor, forthrightness, and commitment building? All the executives failed to walk their talk, and all were unaware of their own inconsistency. When I pointed out the gap between action and intention, most saw it at once. Most were surprised that they hadn't seen it before. Most were quick to recognize inconsistency in others, but their lack of awareness with regard to their own inconsistency was systematic.

I know of only one way to get at these inconsistencies, and that is to focus on them. In the Acme case, the CEO managed to ignore the fact that the survey results didn't compute: on the one hand, employees said they were proud to work for the company and described management as caring; on the other, they doubted management's candor and competence. How could they hold both views? How could they be proud to work for a company whose managers were ineffective and inconsistent?

The CEO did not stop to explore any of these contradictions before embarking on corrective action. Had he done so, he might have discovered that the employees felt strong job satisfaction precisely *because* management never asked them to accept personal responsibility for Acme's poor competitive performance. Employees could safely focus their skepticism on top management because they had learned to depend on top management for their welfare. They claimed to value empowerment when in reality they valued dependence. They claimed commitment to the company when in reality they were committed only to the principle that management should make all the tough decisions, guarantee their employment, and pay them fairly. This logic made sense to employees, but it was *not* the kind of commitment that management had in mind.

None of these issues was ever discussed with employees, and none was raised in the leadership workshops. No effort was made to explore the concept of loyalty that permitted, indeed encouraged, managers to think one thing and say another. No attempt was made to help employees understand the role they played in the "culture of blame" that they'd named in the survey as one of their chief concerns. Above all, no one tried to untangle the defensive logic that contributed so mightily to these inconsistencies and that so badly needed critical examination. In fact, when I asked the management team why they had not discussed these questions, one person told me, "Frankly, until you started asking these questions, it just didn't occur to us. I see your point, but trying to talk to our people about this could be awfully messy. We're really trying to be *positive* here, and this would just stir things up."

The Acme story is a very common one: lots of energy is expended with little lasting progress. Employee surveys like the one Acme conducted—and like most other forms of leader-subordinate communication—have a fundamentally antimanagement bias whenever they deal with double-loop issues. They encourage employees *not* to reflect on their own behavior and attitudes. By assigning all the responsibility for fixing problems to management, they encourage managers *not* to relinquish the top-down, command-and-control mind-set that prevents empowerment.

The employees at Acme, like the 40 supervisors who were wined and dined for their TQM accomplishments, will continue to do what's asked of them as long as they feel adequately rewarded. They will follow the rules, but they will not take initiative, they will not take risks, and they are very unlikely to engage in double-loop learning.

In short, they will not adopt the new behaviors and frames of reference so critical to keeping their companies competitive.

Over the last few years, I have come in contact with any number of companies struggling with this transition from command-and-control hierarchy to employee empowerment and organizational learning, and every one of them is its own worst enemy. Managers embrace the language of intrinsic motivation but fail to see how firmly mired in the old extrinsic world their communications actually are. This is the second explicit way in which corporate communications contribute to nonlearning.

Take the case of the 1,200-person operations division of what I'll call Europabank, where employee commitment to customer service was about to become a matter of survival. The bank's CEO had decided to spin off the division, and its future depended on its ability to *earn* customer loyalty. Europabank's CEO felt confident that the employees could become more market-oriented. Because he knew they would have to take more initiative and risk, he created small project groups to work out all the implementation details and get employees to buy into the new mission. He was pleased with the way the organization was responding.

The vice president for human resources was not so pleased. He worried that the buy-in wasn't genuine and that his boss was overly optimistic. Not wanting to be negative, however, he kept his misgivings to himself.

In order to assess what was really going on here, I needed to know more about the attitudes behind the CEO's behavior. I asked him for some written examples of how he would answer employee concerns about the spin-off. What would he say to allay their doubts and build their commitment? Here are two samples of what he wrote:

- "If the employees express fear about the new plan because the 'old' company guaranteed employment, say: 'The new organization will do its utmost to guarantee employment and better prospects for growth. I promise that.'"

- "If the employees express fear that they are not used to dealing with the market approach, say: 'I promise you will get the education you need, and I will ensure that appropriate actions are rewarded.'"

When these very situations later arose and he made these very statements to employees, their reactions were positive. They felt that the CEO really cared about them.

But look at the confusion of messages and roles. If the CEO means to give these employees a sense of their own power over their own professional fate—and that was his stated intent—then why emphasize instead what *he* will do for *them*? Each time he said, "I promise you," the CEO undermined his own goal of creating internal commitment, intrinsic motivation, and genuine empowerment.

He might have begun to generate real buy-in by pointing out to employees that their wishes were unreasonable. They want management to deal with their fears and reassure them that everything will turn out for the best. They want management to take responsibility for a challenge that is theirs to face. In a market-driven business, the CEO cannot possibly give the guarantees these employees want. The employees see the CEO as caring when he promises to protect and reward them. Unfortunately, this kind of caring disempowers, and someday it will hurt both the employees and the company.

Once employees base their motivation on extrinsic factors—the CEO's promises—they are much less likely to take chances, question established policies and practices, or explore the territory that lies beyond the company vision as defined by management. They are much less likely to learn.

Externally committed employees believe that management manipulates them and see loyalty as allowing the manipulation to take place. They will give honest responses to a direct question or a typical employee survey because they will be glad to tell management what's wrong. They will see it as a loyal act. What they are *not* likely to do is examine the risky issues surrounding their dependence, their ambivalence, and their avoidance of personal responsibility. Employees will commit to TQM, for example, if they believe that their compensation is just and that their managers are fair and trustworthy. However, these conditions, like the commitment they produce, come from an outside source: management.

This is external commitment, and external commitment harnesses external motivation. The energy available for work derives from extrinsic factors like good pay, well-designed jobs, and management promises. Individuals whose commitment and motivation are external depend on their managers to give them the incentive to work.

I recently watched a videotape of the CEO of a large airline meeting with relatively upper-level managers. The CEO repeatedly emphasized the importance of individual empowerment at all levels of the organization. At one point in the tape, a young manager identified a problem that top managers at the home office had prevented him from resolving. The CEO thanked the man and then asked him to go directly to the senior vice president who ran the department in question and raise the issue again.

In the meantime, he said, he would pave the way. By implication, he encouraged all the managers present to take the initiative and come to him if they encountered bureaucratic barriers.

I watched this video with a group of some 80 senior executives. All but one praised the CEO for empowering the young manager. The single dissenter wondered out loud about the quality of the empowerment, which struck him as entirely external, entirely dependent on the action of the CEO.

I agreed with that lonely voice. The CEO could have opened a window into genuine empowerment for the young manager by asking a few critical questions: What had the young man done to communicate his sense of disempowerment to those who blocked him? What fears would doing so have triggered? How could the organization redesign itself to give young managers the freedom and safety to take such initiatives? For that matter, the CEO could have asked these same questions of his senior vice presidents.

By failing to explore the deeper issues—and by failing to encourage his managers to do the same—all the CEO did was promise to lend the young manager some high-level executive power and authority the next time he had a problem. In other words, the CEO built external commitment and gave his manager access to it. What he did *not* do was encourage the young man to build permanent empowerment for himself on the basis of his own insights, abilities, and prerogatives.

Companies that hope to reap the rewards of a committed, empowered workforce have to learn to stop kidding themselves. External commitment, positive thinking at any price, employees protected from the consequences and even the knowledge of cause and effect— this mind-set may produce superficial honesty and single-loop learning, but it will never yield the kind of learning that might actually help a company change. The reason is quite simply that for companies to change, employees must take an active role not only in describing the faults of others but also in drawing out the truth about their own behavior and motivation. In my experience, moreover, employees dig deeper and harder into the truth when the task of scrutinizing the organization includes taking a good look at their own roles, responsibilities, and potential contributions to corrective action.

The problem is not that employees run away from this kind of organizational self-examination. The problem is that no one asks it of them. Managers seem to attach no importance to employees' feelings, defenses, and inner conflicts. Moreover, leaders focus so earnestly on "positive" values—employee satisfaction, upbeat attitude, high morale—that it would strike them as destructive to make demands on employee self-awareness.

But this emphasis on being positive is plainly counterproductive. First, it overlooks the critical role that dissatisfaction, low morale, and negative attitudes can play— often *should* play—in giving an accurate picture of organizational reality, especially with regard to threatening or sensitive issues. (For example, if employees are helping to eliminate their own jobs, why should we expect or encourage them to display high morale or disguise their mixed feelings?) Second, it condescendingly assumes that employees can only function in a cheerful world, even if the cheer is false. We make no such assumption about senior executives. We expect leaders to stand up and take their punches like adults, and we recognize that their best performance is often linked to shaky morale, job insecurity, high levels of frustration, and a vigilant focus on negatives. But leaders have a tendency to treat everyone below the top, including many of their managers, like members of a more fragile race, who can be productive only if they are contented.

Now, there is nothing wrong with contented people, if contentment is the only goal. My research suggests it is possible to achieve quite respectable productivity with middling commitment and morale. The key is a system of external compensation and job security that employees consider fair. In such a system, superficial answers to critical questions produce adequate results, and no one demands more.

But the criteria for effectiveness and responsibility have risen sharply in recent years and will rise more sharply still in the decades to come. A generation ago, business wanted employees to do exactly what they were told, and company leadership bought their acquiescence with a system of purely extrinsic rewards. Extrinsic motivation had fairly narrow boundaries—defined by phrases like "That's not my job"—but it did produce acceptable results with a minimum of complication.

Today, facing competitive pressures an earlier generation could hardly have imagined, managers need employees who think constantly and creatively about the needs of the organization. They need employees with as much *intrinsic* motivation and as deep a sense of organizational stewardship as any company executive. To bring this about, corporate communications must demand more of everyone involved. Leaders and subordinates alike—those who ask and those who answer—must all begin struggling with a new level of self-awareness, candor, and responsibility.

Originally published in July–August 1994
Reprint 94401

Coevolving

At Last, a Way to Make Synergies Work

KATHLEEN M. EISENHARDT AND
D. CHARLES GALUNIC

Executive Summary

THE PROMISE OF SYNERGY is the prime rationale for the existence of the multibusiness corporation. Yet for most corporations, the 1+1=3 arithmetic of cross-business synergies doesn't add up.

Companies that do achieve synergistic success use a corporate strategic process called *coevolving*; they routinely change the web of collaborative links among businesses to exploit fresh opportunities for synergies and drop deteriorating ones. The term *coevolution* originated in biology. It refers to the way two or more ecologically interdependent species become intertwined over time. As these species adapt to their environment, they also adapt to one another.

Today's multibusiness companies need to take their cue from biology to survive: They should assume that links among businesses are temporary and that the number of connections—not just their content—matters. Rather than plan collaborative strategy from the top, as traditional companies do, corporate executives in coevolving companies should simply set the context and then let collaboration (and competition) emerge from business units.

Incentives, too, are different than they are in traditional companies. Coevolving companies reward business units for individual performance, not for collaboration. So collaboration occurs only when two business-unit managers both believe that a link makes sense for their respective businesses, not because collaboration per se is useful. Managers in coevolving companies also need to recognize the importance of business systems that support the process: frequent data-focused meetings among business-unit leaders, external metrics to gauge individual business performance, and incentives that favor self-interest.

Capturing cross-business synergies is at the heart of corporate strategy—indeed, the promise of synergy is a prime rationale for the existence of the multibusiness corporation. Yet synergies are notoriously challenging to capture. Shell's initial attempt to launch a common credit card across Europe failed. Allegis, United Airlines' bid to build synergies in related travel businesses like hotels and airlines, was dismantled. Amazon.com has yet to see significant synergies from its PlanetAll acquisition, which was supposed to drive additional sales by linking to people's Rolodex of family and friends. The truth is, for most corporations, the 1+1=3 arithmetic of cross-business synergies does not add up.

So how do the companies that actually achieve synergies do it? Their managers have mastered a corporate strategic process called *coevolving*. These managers routinely change the web of collaborative links—everything from information exchanges to shared assets to multibusiness strategies—among businesses. The result is a shifting web of relationships that exploits fresh opportunities for synergies and drops deteriorating ones. (See "Disney versus Sony: Contrasting Cases in Patching and Coevolution" at the end of this article.)

The term *coevolution* originated in biology. It refers to successive changes among two or more ecologically interdependent but unique species such that their evolutionary trajectories become intertwined over time. As these species adapt to their environment, they also adapt to one another. The result is an ecosystem of partially interdependent species that adapt together. This interdependence is often symbiotic (each species helps the other), but it can also be commensalist (one species uses the other). Competitive interdependence can emerge as well: one species may drive out the other, or both species may evolve into distinct, noncompetitive niches. Interdependence can change, too, such as when external factors like the climate or geology shift.

A classic example of symbiotic coevolution is the acacia tree and the *pseudomyrmex* ant species. Ants need acacias for nectar and shelter. Acacias depend on the ants stinging to protect them from herbivores. Over time, the acacia has evolved to make it easy for the ants to hollow out thorns for shelter and to have access to its flowers. Similarly, the ants have evolved into a shape that makes it easier to enter the acacia flower. Together, the species are better off than they would be if they didn't collaborate.

Scholars from many disciplines have recognized that biological coevolution is just one kind of complex adaptive system. Recently, computer simulations have uncovered general laws of how these systems work, including social systems such as multicountry economies and multibusiness corporations. These laws reveal nonlinear effects such as leverage points with disproportionate impact on the entire system. They show how the number of connections can affect the agility of a system. And they indicate that complex adaptive systems are most effective when intelligence is decentralized. More generally, these laws are consistent with the notion that multibusiness corporations are coevolving ecosystems.

So what does all that mean for today's multibusiness companies? In essence, they need to take their cue from nature and approach cross-business synergies with a very different mind-set. Managers at coevolving companies assume that links among businesses are temporary. They think "Velcro organization." They also recognize that the number of connections—not just their content—matters. So they manage the tension between fewer links for agility and more links for efficiency. While traditional corporate managers plan collaborative strategy from the top, corporate executives in coevolving companies don't try to control or even predict it. They set the context and then let collaboration (and competition) emerge from business units. Incentives are different, too. Coevolving companies reward business units for individual performance, not for collaboration. Thus, collaboration occurs only when two business-unit managers both believe that a link makes sense for their respective businesses, not because collaboration per se is useful. Finally, managers in coevolving companies recognize the importance of business systems: frequent data-focused meetings among business-unit leaders, external metrics to gauge individual business performance, and incentives that favor self-interest. (See the table "Traditional Collaboration Versus Coevolution.")

Coevolving is a particularly crucial strategic process in new-economy corporations, where higher-velocity markets drive managers to keep individual businesses small enough to adapt but intense competition demands that they maintain economies of scope and rapid cross-business learning. Not surprisingly, many leading corpo-

Traditional Collaboration vs. Coevolution

	Traditional Collaboration	Coevolution
Form of collaboration	Frozen links among static businesses	Shifting webs among evolving businesses
Objectives	Efficiency and economies of scope	Growth, agility, and economies of scope
Internal dynamics	Collaborate	Collaborate and compete
Focus	Content of collaboration	Content and number of collaborative links
Corporate role	Drive collaboration	Set collaborative context
Business role	Execute collaboration	Drive and execute collaboration
Incentive	Varied	Self-interest, based on individual business-unit performance
Business metrics	Performance against budget, the preceding year, or sister-business performance	Performance against competitors in growth, share, and profits

rations with significant Internet businesses like Sun, Schwab, and Hewlett-Packard coevolve. Since even pre-IPO companies in the new economy often have multiple businesses, very young firms like eye-care specialist NovaMed coevolve as well. And finally, coevolving is crucial for knowledge-intensive corporations like consultancy Booz-Allen & Hamilton and product design firm IDEO, which constantly share learning throughout their organizations.

Our ideas about coevolving developed from a decade of research into successful corporate strategy in intensely competitive, fast-moving industries. Coevolution in natural ecosystems, we found, looks a lot like the collaborative webs within corporations that achieve significant multibusiness synergies. And both of these resemble the external ecosystems that link corporations together in webs of alliances. More generally, the disciplines of biology and complexity yield important insights into how superior corporate strategy—inside and outside the corporation—happens in dynamic markets.

Shift Collaborative Webs

In traditional corporations, the web of collaborations among businesses often freezes into fixed patterns. Business units share intangible resources such as brands, physical resources such as manufacturing facilities, or organizational capabilities such as product development. Once the patterns are established, they're not revisited regularly. By contrast, managers in coevolving corporations frequently reconnect the links among businesses. Some links last a long time, others are much shorter. And while some links lead to predicted synergies, others open up unanticipated ones.

GE Capital is an example of a company that reconnects its collaborative webs. GE Capital was launched with collaborative links to GE's consumer businesses, such as refrigerators and dishwashers. As time went on, GE Capital gained enough scale and expertise to offer its financing services to GE's more sophisticated industrial products businesses like power plants and jet engines. The collaborative web shifted more toward these areas. The combination of products and innovative financing fed the growth of both GE Capital and the industrial products businesses. Eventually, GE Capital became its own web of interconnected businesses, like specialty insurance and credit card operations, by developing common acquisition procedures and sharing customers. As a result of that changing collaborative web, GE managers created synergistic growth beyond what static collaborations could have achieved.

Another company we'll call OfficeSys provides a detailed illustration of the types of collaborations that managers at coevolving companies use. Three years ago, OfficeSys was dominated by two large businesses: photocopiers and fax machines. For many years, those businesses had shared optical technologies and product components. As industry price cutting slashed margins, the managers of the two businesses combined their manufacturing and procurement activities. As a result, both were able to cut costs and compete more effectively in their markets. At about the same time in 1997, corporate executives at OfficeSys launched two new businesses around a revolutionary optical scanning technology that captures data for transfer to the Internet. These managers collaborated very informally by trading engineers back and forth in order to share scarce and costly talent. They also collaborated on developing a software protocol standard for data transmission among different Internet-connected devices.

But as is often the case in coevolving companies, the collaborative web evolved. When the two new businesses began to ship products, their managers ended the informal swapping of engineers. The managers of the fax business joined the software standard collaboration. The managers of all four businesses now have a joint advertising campaign to promote their collective brand.

The OfficeSys example is striking because of the variety of collaborations that took place. Some collaborations were major and long term, such as the joint development of common product components. Some were modest and transient, like the informal trading of engineers. Some were focused on creating revenue, like the software protocol initiative and brand building. Some drove down costs, like shared manufacturing. And they occurred all along the value chain, from R&D to marketing. Because of their coevolutionary efforts, OfficeSys's managers strengthened their businesses in the maturing photocopier and fax markets and grew their businesses in the emerging Internet appliances markets.

What drives managers to reconnect their collaborative webs? Sometimes it's changes in the market, pure and simple. For example, increased cost pressures forced managers at OfficeSys to expand manufacturing links between their mature businesses. Sometimes it's changes in the business units themselves. Managers pursue new directions, adjust to the changing business roles of sister divisions, or simply grow their businesses. Most commonly, it's a combination of the two.

NovaMed Eyecare Management, a fast-growing, successful health-care company, is an example of how changes made by an individual business unit can reverberate throughout the larger business group, affecting how other units relate to one another and how they all relate to the market. In 1995, NovaMed's eye-care medical practices throughout the United States were similar. The collaborative relationships among the practices focused on saving costs through common information systems, bulk purchasing, and shared staff.

The doctors in one practice, however, had particularly strong research skills, especially in refractive surgery. They decided to put those skills to use. As the doctors became the innovators and new laser technology for eye surgery was approved by the FDA, the pattern of collaboration shifted. Sharing resources to lower costs was still important, but the transmission of surgical innovations became far more crucial. That is, doctors at the research-driven practice pioneered new surgical procedures and then broadcast them throughout NovaMed.

In 1998, NovaMed launched a new kind of business, one that conducted clinical trials of surgical equipment and their related procedures for medical device companies. The doctors at the research-based practice worked closely with this new business, which strengthened their ability to pioneer leading-edge surgical techniques. Some of the more research-oriented doctors within the other practices also began collaborating

In coevolving companies, e-businesses compete with their bricks-and-mortar counterparts and new technologies compete with established ones.

with the clinical trials business. As a result, NovaMed was able to build the critical mass of participating doctors and patients necessary for meaningful clinical trials. Not surprisingly, the company has grown over 60% during the first half of 1999 compared with 1998, and it went through a successful IPO. More to the point, NovaMed's practices have moved much faster and with greater medical skill than competitors into refractive surgery, one of the hottest growth segments in health care.

Bring the Market Inside

Managers at companies that follow the traditional rules for collaboration avoid internal competition on the grounds that it devastates teamwork, wastes resources, and cannibalizes existing products and businesses. By contrast, managers at coevolving companies let collaboration and competition coexist. E-businesses compete with their bricks-and-mortar counterparts, new technologies compete with established ones, and so on. While senior managers don't actively seek out competition, they don't discourage it if it occurs naturally as the result of alternative technologies, business models, distribution channels, and the like. Just as the distinction between friend and foe is blurring in the alliance webs outside the corporation, it is also blurring on the inside.

An exemplar of such thinking is Hewlett-Packard. For decades, the tension between competition and cooperation has helped HP thrive. A classic example involves the desk- and laser-jet printing technologies. Eventually the two businesses evolved into different market niches and became enormous businesses in their own right, but for several years they competed for the same customers. The company's managers knew they could not predict how the market would unfold, so they let the two compete until it became clear whether one would dominate or whether the businesses would diverge into viable market niches. Had the managers at HP squelched this competition by choosing one technology over the other, they would have lost out on a collective $15 billion business opportunity. Recently, that same kind of competition has

emerged between HP's UNIX and NT computing businesses. Initially, UNIX was the primary business. Then
NT looked to be the winner. Now with the rise of Linux
and repeated NT delays, UNIX is resurgent. The result of
such competition is that HP can win regardless of how
the market unfolds.

Letting internal competition flourish is particularly
important in the Internet world. Managers who think in
terms of coevolution let Net businesses compete with
established ones. A good example is Siebel Systems, a
"best of breed" provider of enterprise software for sales
and marketing. Siebel's managers didn't let the usual
concerns about channel conflict keep them from quickly
entering e-commerce. In fact, Siebel's new subsidiary,
Sales.com, initially targeted the same customers as the
existing business—major global corporations with complex selling requirements. Early on, the two diverged;
Sales.com sold Web-hosted application products directly
to individual salespeople in these corporations, and the
traditional business concentrated on selling software for
the entire sales force to senior executives. Sales.com's
products turned out to be most appealing to small and
mid-sized companies that found Web-hosting to be an
attractive alternative to enterprise software resident on
their own IT equipment. By letting competition unfold,
Siebel managers figured out how to play the Internet
game well before other ERP companies like PeopleSoft,
while keeping their established business successful.

Balance the Number of Links

Traditional corporations focus on picking the right collaborations. By contrast, coevolving companies recognize that the *number* of collaborative ties is often just as

significant as the kinds of collaborations. They balance the tension between too many links that restrict adaptation and too few that miss important opportunities for synergies.

A terrific example is Vail Ski Resorts. When the group formed in a 1997 merger, the rationale was to gain extensive synergies by tightly linking the four member resorts—Vail, Breckenridge, Keystone, and Beaver Creek—with numerous collaborations, particularly branding under the Vail name. It was a classic, top-down plan to create synergies—with the usual sub-par results. Vacationers wanted unique resort experiences, not four "would-be Vail" destinations. Once senior managers cut back on these connections, they could more freely adapt their resorts to their evolving markets. For example, Breckenridge's location next to a classic mining town has particular appeal for European skiers seeking a "Western" experience. Breckenridge's managers capitalized on this attraction by introducing unique features that appeal to these skiers, such as longer-stay vacation packages. Loosening the connections also allowed Vail Resorts' managers to figure out, over time, the right number of connections among the resorts. Today the resort group collaborates—by choice—in only a few high-payoff areas: supplies procurement, integrated information systems, and interchangeable lift ticketing.

When markets become dynamic and agility matters most, businesses need fewer collaborative connections.

As a general rule, more links among businesses make sense when markets are stable. In such circumstances, economies of scope dominate. Disney's approach to the Internet illustrates this principle. In general, Disney's businesses are highly connected. But the company's managers intentionally entered the volatile Internet world with businesses that were only weakly tied together. Their Infoseek business, in fact, was not even fully owned. Figuring that the old business models might not make sense, managers wanted plenty of freedom to evolve in and even shape whatever the emerging market spaces would be. They understood that agility—not control—matters in fast-moving markets. Yet now that the Internet markets are more crystallized, Disney's managers have aggressively linked their Internet plays with one another and other parts of Disney. Once again, economies of scope drive Disney's thinking. They bought the rest of Infoseek, combined it with other Internet businesses such as Disney Travel Online into a single business (Go.com), made their content Web sites accessible from a single portal (Go Network), and created new links to established businesses like ESPN. Of course, the jury is still out on whether they connected too soon in the volatile I-world.

By contrast, when markets become dynamic and agility matters most, businesses need fewer connections in order to adapt. Consider the British Broadcasting Company. For years, the radio station, television broadcast, and television production businesses were tightly linked, even to the point of cross-subsidization. Radio, in particular, was viewed as the decidedly unglamorous cash cow. But, in one of the surprises of the Internet, radio's prospects have changed. Why? Many people shut off their televisions and turn on their radios for background entertainment while they surf the Web. So BBC has loosened the links among its businesses to let radio evolve more freely in the higher-velocity, less predictable Internet space.

Uncover the High-Leverage Links

Especially in fast-paced markets, managers don't have time to oversee a lot of collaborative initiatives. So it's crucial to figure out what links are sensible, identify the high-payoff ones, and forget the rest. Typically, the highest-payoff links can be leverage points with disproportionate synergies.

A great example is the U.S. multichain retailer Dayton Hudson. There are only a few collaborative links between the rapidly growing Target chain and upscale retailers Marshall Field's and Dayton's. But senior managers have located a simple link that gives them a lot of leverage: regular exchange of fashion information. Target, in particular, has benefited. Its managers learn about fashion trends much sooner than competitors by paying attention to the upscale retailers, whose buyers spot trends early through their contacts with leading fashion designers. (For example, Target got wind of the recent "gray craze" from other Dayton Hudson managers and tailored its apparel and home furnishings accordingly.) This link helped Target managers to reposition the chain as "hip fashion at a low price" and achieve double-digit sales and profit growth that buried competitors like Kmart and J.C. Penney. So does this success mean that Target should add more links? Absolutely not. In fact, for Target, more links such as common buyers might actually slow the retailer down, raise costs, and lower the synergistic value of the businesses. In other words, fewer links—targeted at the right content—can, counterintuitively, create more synergies.

The exact location of these high-leverage links depends upon a company's resources, the relatedness of its businesses, and its strategic position. Take Cisco and

Ascend, two competing stars of the turbulent networking industry. Given the pace and uncertainty of that industry, it makes sense for managers at both companies to focus on just a few collaborative areas. But because their circumstances are different, their managers have chosen different links. Cisco has a huge market cap, which makes acquisitions relatively affordable. Managers have

The most effective decision makers are those at the business-unit level, where strategic perspective meets operating savvy.

used that advantage brilliantly: they have developed a shared acquisition process—from target identification through due diligence to integration—that capitalizes on learning-curve effects of acquisitions throughout the corporation. Managers use this shared process to make frequent acquisitions that supplement in-house R&D and open up new product areas. In effect, Cisco's managers transfer R&D risk to venture capitalists and then scoop up the winners. Ascend, in comparison, was launched well after Cisco. When the company was young, its managers couldn't afford acquisitions to open up new product areas. But they needed to move very fast with a low profile to stay well ahead of Cisco. So Ascend's managers concentrated their cross-business collaborations on aggressively sharing software and other product components across businesses. This collaborative link preserved precious financial resources, accelerated time to market and, at least initially, kept Ascend off Cisco's radar screen.

Lay the Foundation

Understanding the essentials—frequently reconnect the relationships among businesses, blur collaboration and competition, manage the number of connections, and uncover high-leverage links—is crucial for companies that hope to coevolve. But it's not enough. There is an underlying foundation of structures and processes that managers must build if coevolution is to work.

LET BUSINESS UNITS RULE

A cornerstone of that foundation is letting heads of business units determine where and when to collaborate. If corporate managers take the lead, they often do not understand the nuances of the businesses. They naively see synergies that aren't there. They tend to overestimate the benefits of collaboration and underestimate its costs. Conversely, if junior managers take the lead, they lack the strategic perspective to pick the best opportunities. They may spot good opportunities for collaboration, but they rarely uncover the best ones. Thus, the most effective decision makers are those at the business-unit level, where strategic perspective meets operating savvy.

The locus of decision making at General Electric is a prime example. General managers of GE's businesses have regular meetings to search for cross-business synergies. These meetings typically include managers from related businesses where synergies could be expected. They engage in what is called "receiver-based communication." That is, they share information about their activities, and interested managers from other businesses (the "receivers") follow up as they see appropriate. Even though senior executives may suggest areas of collaboration and individual business managers are expected to attend the meetings, nobody is forced to collaborate. Business general managers make the collaborative calls.

That doesn't mean that corporate-level managers have no role in cross-business collaboration. On the contrary, senior executives create the context in which that collaboration can happen. They act as "pollinators" of ideas as they travel among businesses. They stage modern-day bazaars that bring business-level managers together to talk and to perhaps find collaborative opportunities. They determine the lineup of businesses within the corporation by patching businesses against market opportunities so that effective collaboration can emerge. They ensure that each business is strong enough to be an attractive partner. They also foster a culture of information sharing by assigning synergy managers within individual business units. These executives may even suggest particular collaborations for individual businesses. But they don't force collaboration. (For more on the executive roles, see "Patching, Coevolving, and the New Corporate Strategy" at the end of this article.)

BUILD THE MULTIBUSINESS TEAM

Another cornerstone of coevolution is the multibusiness team—the group of business unit heads that orchestrates collaborations among their businesses. The key to making these teams work well is frequent group meetings. In the most successful coevolving companies, these meetings happen at least monthly and are "don't miss" events. The content of these meetings is a run-through of real-time internal operating numbers and external market statistics, as well as a qualitative discussion of shared interests such as competitors' moves, customer feedback, and technology developments. The meetings are fact-focused and pragmatic. Often managers discuss a specific strategic issue facing one or more of the businesses. Since travel can be a problem, effective teams rely a lot on videoconferences. They add fun to the mix, too. Eli Lilly's managers, for example, organize some meetings in enticing locations like London, where they give executives time to shop, visit local pubs, or sightsee.

The most obvious effect of frequent meetings is that business heads become acquainted with opportunities for collaboration. But just as important, they weave the social fabric of familiarity and trust that supports effective collaboration. (See "The Power of Multibusiness Teams" at the end of this article.)

Consider Time Warner. Its managers are notoriously uncollaborative, and compared with other media giants, the corporation as a whole has not gained much synergistic value from its businesses. However, managers from the Turner Sports group, *Sports Illustrated* magazine, and the sports wing of HBO started meeting often. As a result, they have learned about one another's needs and resources. These meetings have led to several collaborative efforts, including the Turner Games boxing events. These were organized by Turner Sports, promoted and broadcast on HBO, and covered by *Sports Illustrated*.

A more subtle, albeit well-known, effect of these meetings is the emergence of roles. For example, at Vail Ski Resorts, their weekly meetings helped managers shape the business roles of their own ski areas in relation to one another. Vail's role, for example, has become the "capital of skiing," while Breckenridge evolved into the "Western" experience. Establishing very clear turf boundaries helped the managers of those businesses communicate more clearly and collaborate more effectively by lowering political tension and clarifying opportunities. The result is that Vail Ski Resorts competes very successfully against competitors like Intrawest because of its distinctly focused ski experiences and effective synergies.

Finally, frequent meetings can lead to the emergence of a shared intuition. As managers regularly review the operating performances and markets of all the businesses together, they develop a common understanding—a gut sense—of the patterns shaping their industry. Because these meetings focus managers on factual data, their shared intuition remains tightly linked with shifting realities and helps multibusiness teams identify the best collaborations quickly.

But in certain situations (notably related businesses facing a small number of competitors), that shared intuition can deepen into a multibusiness strategy that goes beyond particular business roles to include coordinated pricing, technology and product road maps, and customer segmentation. This happened at a global computing company we'll call Cruising. The managers of Cruising's primary computing businesses instituted bimonthly meetings to track their turbulent industry. Over time, the different businesses developed distinct roles and a shared multibusiness strategy. For example, one business was in the fastest-growing, highest-margin segment of the industry. So it became the golden goose, and the company's overall strategy was to protect and grow this business. A second business took on the workhorse role. It was the largest business and sold the greatest number of products, so it contributed manufacturing volume and routines for many basic business processes. It also relayed information about low-end competitors attacking the golden goose from below. A third business competed in a small, high-margin segment of the industry. That business helped several other Cruising businesses to gain sales by promising delivery of these short-supply, high-quality products if the customer bought other products from Cruising. As a result of this multibusiness strategy, Cruising became the industry's company to beat.

GET THE INCENTIVES RIGHT

If coevolving requires multibusiness teams that can quickly identify and execute collaborative opportunities, then the incentives for business-unit heads must reward collaboration. Right? Wrong. Business-unit managers who coevolve their businesses are rewarded for self-interest, *not* for collaboration. That is, they are rewarded primarily for their individual business performance. That performance is measured externally against key competitors—not internally against planned, preceding year, or sister-business performance—with the metrics typically being a mix of growth, profit, and market share. The ultimate reward, as in professional sports, is being on the team. So, for example, the manager of a business in a very competitive market does not need to post the same numbers as a manager who competes with better strategic position. Both are expected to excel in their own markets. If they do, they are on the team and are well compensated. If not, they're off.

Rewarding self-interest works because it's simple. It turns the attention of business-unit managers to the most important thing they need to do—win in their own markets. By contrast, mixed incentives (some group, some individual) confuse and demotivate people. Self-interest works for another reason, too. It makes market realities, not friendship, the basis of collaboration. In particular, it banishes the "good people collaborate and bad people don't" thinking that leads to ineffective collaboration. Finally, rewarding self-interest works because win-win collaborations usually create the biggest synergistic pie for the corporation, even when individual businesses get unequal slices. It's true that occasionally an opportunity that's great for the corporation is missed because it was not so good for the businesses—but in dynamic markets, worrying about the corporate optimum is just too slow.

Individual-based incentives run counter to the culture of companies that place a high value on collective behavior. But these companies pay a price. Take Mitsubishi. Mitsubishi outwardly has some of the infrastructure of coevolving companies, such as regular Friday lunch meetings for business-unit heads. The collectivist culture at Mitsubishi, however, has led to some ineffective collaborations. For example, *keiretsu* members purchased steel inside Mitsubishi even though better deals were available from outside suppliers. Similarly, fellow keiretsu member Kirin protected its premium beer business from internal competition and subsequently lost to outsider Asahi in key growth segments of the Japanese beer market.

Of course, even in the best coevolving companies, collaborative efforts may not happen when they should. Rather than switch to rewarding collaboration, coevolving executives look for alternatives: they improve information flow so that managers can see collaborative opportunities better; repatch closely aligned businesses together into larger business segments; or repair businesses that others may be avoiding because they are ineffective. What coevolving managers *don't* do is reward collaboration.

Is Coevolving Right for Your Company?

Capturing cross-business synergies is an essential part of corporate strategy. Yet many managers collaborate in too many areas or for too long, or they focus on the wrong opportunities. They forget that, especially in high-velocity markets, there's not a lot of time to collaborate. They neglect to update their collaborative links as businesses and markets emerge, grow, split, and combine. Of course, some managers simply ignore cross-business synergies, an approach that often beats poor collaboration. But it also defeats the point of the multibusiness corporation. Coevolving is a better alternative.

Coevolving is a subtle strategic process. In fact, it's a bit counterintuitive—build collaborative teams and yet reward self-interest, let competition flourish, don't worry too much about efficiency, collaborate less to gain more. Coevolving turns the corporation into an ecosystem with corporate strategy in the hands of business-unit managers. But it is precisely this oblique thinking that gives coevolving companies a competitive edge.

Disney Versus Sony: Contrasting Cases in Patching and Coevolution

IN THE MID-1990s, Sony scored a box-office hit with *Men in Black*, while Disney had a similar box-office success with *The Lion King*. *Men in Black* grossed more money in its first weekend than almost any other film in history. For Sony, the $600 million box-office and video revenues were much of its success story. For Disney, those revenue sources were just the opening chapter. Disney's managers also released more than 150 kinds of *Lion King* merchandise (pencil cases, dolls, T-shirts, and so forth), turned the soundtrack into a musical sequel called *Rhythm of the Pride Lands*, and produced a video entitled *Simba's Pride*. The total take was approximately $3 billion. Disney also introduced *Lion King* themes at existing resorts and ultimately at its new Animal Kingdom theme park.

Most people understand the 1+1=3 arithmetic of Disney's collaboration, which funnels the same content into multiple media businesses. But few people recognize that Disney's managers use different collaborative patterns with different products. *Beauty and the Beast* became a play on Broadway, for example, whereas *Toy Story* was turned into a video game, and *The Little Mermaid* became a television show. Even fewer people understand that Disney's managers engage in many kinds of collaborative efforts that change over time. Managers of Disney World and the Big Red Boat cruise line collaborate on joint vacation packages to boost revenues for both businesses, for example. EuroDisney executives share knowledge about hotel management and ticket pricing with other resort managers. ESPN managers work with the Internet businesses to share sports content and with the theme parks to launch ESPN restaurants. Touchstone Studios occasionally shares actors with animated films. Thus, Disney's managers have effectively patched together a changing quilt of entertainment businesses like theme parks, movie studios, retail stores, and broadcast networks. Simultaneously, they have created the corporate context (like synergy managers in each business, corporate Imagineers, and the Disney Dimensions program) that permits the coevolving mix of collaboration among these businesses. (For more on how Disney creates synergies, see "Common Sense and Conflict: An Interview with Disney's Michael Eisner," in HBR January–February 2000.)

By contrast, Sony's managers have not patched businesses such as theme parks, publishing, and retail outlets into their company, even though other entertainment companies have found that they're important for creating corporate synergies. They also have some businesses that on the surface seem synergistic but aren't. For example, Sony's Walkman products obviously depend on media content, but consumers are unlikely to listen to Sony-produced music just because they have a Walkman. Further, Sony's managers have been less effective in capturing the collaborative opportunities they do have because of long-distance relationships between business heads in Tokyo and New York. Not surprisingly, then, Disney has outperformed Sony in many one-on-one matchups like *The Lion King* versus *Men in Black*—and more generally in the creation of corporate value in the entertainment industry.

The Power of Multibusiness Teams

IN TRADITIONAL CORPORATE STRATEGY, the multibusiness team—the group of business-unit managers that oversees synergies among businesses—simply doesn't exist. And yet, it is an organizational requirement for coevolutionary companies. The team's primary job is to orchestrate the shifting collaborative web among the businesses. Most of the time, these managers represent their own businesses. But we have also observed that business-unit heads often temporarily assume functional perspectives. Those who have experience in engineering or marketing, for example, take on those perspectives, especially when the team is discussing multibusiness strategy. Members also take on other, equally distinctive roles—devil's advocate, conservative, innovator, to name a few—which can further enhance the team's effectiveness.

The multibusiness team is powerful because it can add significant value to the corporation beyond the sum of the businesses. Without the teams, individual business managers have difficulty finding collaborative links, developing the social relationships with other business heads that facilitate collaboration, and even conceptualizing a collective strategy. The multibusiness team can also create corporate value that the market cannot duplicate with a portfolio of investments. The market cannot reproduce either the deep understanding of collaborative possibilities that can exist among team members or the underlying social structure that enables effective collaborations over time. Of course, especially in very dynamic markets, many of the best collaborative links are outside the corporation. But even then, the market holds no advantage when multibusiness teams work well together and yet also focus on achieving individual business success.

The key to superior multibusiness teams is great group dynamics: fast decision making with plenty of conflict over content, but also with deep social bonds that limit interpersonal conflict. To create this group process, these teams rely on frequent meetings to build familiarity and trust, data-rich information to develop a shared intuition, and clear turf boundaries so that politicking is kept to a minimum.

Patching, Coevolving, and the New Corporate Strategy

TRADITIONAL CORPORATE STRATEGY CENTERS on establishing defensible strategic positions by setting corporate scope, acquiring or building assets, and weaving synergies among them. The result is sustained competitive advantage. Yet in high-velocity markets, strategic position can quickly erode. In these markets, the strategic *processes* by which managers reconfigure resources to build new strategic positions are more pivotal to corporate performance than any particular strategic position. The new corporate strategy focuses on these freshly defined corporate strategic processes.

One of these processes is patching. Patching is the frequent remapping of businesses to fit changing market opportunities. It involves combining, splitting, exiting, and transferring businesses within the corporation. (For more on the concept of patching, see Kathleen M. Eisenhardt and Shona L. Brown, "Patching: Restitching Business Portfolios in Dynamic Markets," HBR May–June 1999.) A second is coevolving.

With patching, corporate executives set the lineup of businesses within the corporation and keep it aligned with shifting markets. Their key skill is recognizing changing patterns in product and customer segments and in technology road maps. With coevolving, multibusiness teams (the heads of individual businesses working together) drive synergies by reconnecting the collaborative links among businesses as markets and businesses evolve. Their key skill is managing their own group dynamics.

While patching and coevolving are distinct corporate strategic processes, the two are often intertwined. For example, NovaMed's coevolution from purely cost-oriented collaboration among its different medical practices to innovation-oriented collaboration was enhanced when a new clinical-trials business was patched into the company. The new business strengthened the payoff from innovation-based synergies.

Seven Steps to Kick-Start Coevolution

1. Begin by establishing at least monthly, must-attend meetings among business heads that enable them to get to know one another and to see collaborative opportunities.

2. Keep the conversation focused on real-time information about operating basics to build intuition and business roles. Include one or two specific strategic issues within or across businesses.

3. Get rid of "good people collaborate, bad people don't" thinking by rewarding self-interested pursuit of individual business performance against rivals.

4. When collaborative opportunities arise, remember that many managers get stuck on their first idea. Instead, brainstorm to expand the range of possible collaborative tools—from simple information sharing to shared assets to strategy—and collaborative points along the value chain.

5. Realistically analyze the costs and benefits of the most promising options. Remember that benefits usually appear greater than they are.

6. Fine-tune as you go. Up-front analysis is never a substitute for real-time learning.

7. Avoid "collaboration creep." Take the time to cut stale links.

Originally published in January–February 2000
Reprint R00103

Organigraphs

Drawing How Companies Really Work

HENRY MINTZBERG AND

LUDO VAN DER HEYDEN

Executive Summary

WALK INTO ANY ORGANIZATION and you will get a snapshot of the company in action—people and products moving every which way. But ask for a picture of the company and you will be given the org chart, with its orderly little boxes showing just the names and titles of managers.

Now there's a more revealing way to depict the people and operations within an organization—an approach called the *organigraph*. The organigraph is not a chart. It's a map that offers an overview of the company's functions and the ways that people organize themselves at work. Perhaps most important, an organi-graph can help managers see untapped competitive opportunities.

Drawing on the organigraphs they created for about a dozen companies, authors Mintzberg and Van der

Heyden illustrate just how valuable a tool the organigraph is. For instance, one they created for Electrocomponents, a British distributor of electrical and mechanical items, led managers to a better understanding of the company's real expertise—business-to-business relationships. As a result of that insight, the company wisely decided to expand in Asia and to increase its Internet business. As one manager says, "It allowed the company to see all sorts of new possibilities."

With traditional hierarchies vanishing and newfangled—and often quite complex—organizational forms taking their place, people are struggling to understand how their companies work. What parts connect to one another? How should processes and people come together? Whose ideas have to flow where? With their flexibility and realism, organigraphs give managers a new way to answer those questions.

W ALK INTO ANY ORGANIZATION—not the nice, neat managerial offices but the factory, design studio, or sales department—and take a good look. In one corner, a group of people are huddled in debate over a vexing logistics problem. In another, someone is negotiating with a customer halfway around the world on the Internet. Everywhere you look, people and products are moving, crisscrossing this way and that. You get a snapshot of the company in action.

Ask for a picture of the place, however, and chances are you'll be handed the company's org chart, with its orderly little boxes stacked atop one another. The org chart would show you the names and titles of managers, but little else about the company—not its products, processes, or customers—perhaps not even its line of business. Indeed, using an org chart to "view" a company is like using a list of municipal managers to find your way around a city.

The fact is, organizational charts are the picture albums of our companies, but they tell us only that we are mesmerized with management. No wonder they have become so irrelevant in today's world. With traditional hierarchies vanishing, and newfangled—and often quite complex—organizational forms taking their place, people are struggling to understand how their companies work. What parts connect to one another? How should processes and people come together? Whose ideas have to flow where? The answers to those questions not only help individuals understand how they fit into the grand scheme of things but also reveal all sorts of opportunities for competitive advantage.

For the past several years, we have been experimenting with a new way to draw—and thus, see—organizations. We call our approach an *organigraph*, a tip of the hat to the word *organigramme*, the French term for organizational charts. Organigraphs don't eliminate the little boxes altogether. But they do introduce new components called hubs and webs—forms that we believe reflect the varied ways people organize themselves at work today. Organigraphs are more than just pictures; they are also maps. They do not show individuals or positions so much as they provide an overview of a company's territory—its mountains, rivers, and towns, and the roads that connect them.

We have created organigraphs for about a dozen companies and have found that they are much more useful than traditional charts in showing *what* an organization is—why it exists, what it does. Organigraphs have been able to demonstrate *how* a place works, depicting critical interactions among people, products, and information. Moreover, executives have used their organigraphs to stimulate conversations about how best to manage their operations and which strategic options make the most sense, much as hikers use maps to investigate possible routes.

Take a look at the exhibit "Organigraph of a Petrochemical Company." It shows how the company operates like a traditional chain: raw materials are found or purchased, perhaps traded, and then refined and sold. Those activities constitute the main petroleum business. The organigraph also shows how the company's chemicals division connects with this chain in a more iterative, weblike way, drawing out materials from the refinery and feeding them in at another stage, at the retail gas pumps. While the sequential business relationships could very naturally be managed by a centralized planning office, the more weblike ones—with their need for negotiation of transfer prices and the like—may call for a more decentralized approach. Seeing such relationships illustrated

Organigraph of a Petrochemical Company

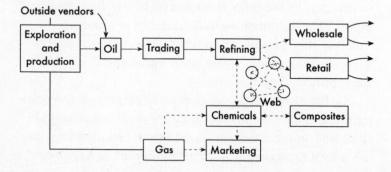

can help a company understand the need for different managerial mind-sets throughout the organization.

That businesses need a new way to depict their organizations is hardly a novel contention. In 1993, an article in *Business Week* suggested that companies begin to replace their org charts with figures that look like starbursts, shamrocks, and pizzas. Some commentators have even suggested that org charts be stood on their heads, putting operating employees on the top and bosses on the bottom. But all turning them upside down would do is provide a better depiction of the senior manager's headache. Organigraphs, instead, offer a new way to look at our companies. They are pictures that show not headaches but real businesses and their opportunities.

The Basic Forms of Organizing

Organigraphs contain two rather conventional components. The first is a *set*. Every organization is a set of items, such as machines or people. Sometimes these items barely connect with one another, and so they remain just that—sets. Parts in a warehouse, for example, wait there as independent items, as do the finished products of a factory before they are shipped off. Many professional service firms, such as law offices, operate as sets, with professionals working almost exclusively with their own clients. The same can be said about the divisions of a conglomerate company or the professors teaching and doing research at a university: all of these function rather independently. They are loosely coupled as a collection, a group, or a portfolio. These sets usually share common resources—facilities, funds, overall management—or else they would not be found in the same organization. But otherwise, they are on their own.

More commonly, though, organizations don't exist to house sets. They exist for purposes of connection. And connection is usually shown by the second conventional form, the *chain*. Materials enter a factory to be transformed into parts, which are combined into subassemblies, which are combined into final assemblies and then shipped to customers. The assembly line in an automobile factory is the prototypical example of this linear connecting process—here, chains prevail. Indeed, chains are so embedded in business imagery that many managers describe their strategies in terms of value chains and their logistics in terms of supply chains.

The preponderance of chains in business thinking is certainly understandable. Because chains are linear, they promote standardization and therefore enhance reliability. They can clarify and systematize the many complex processes that constitute business today. Imagine an automobile factory without chains! But do chains really describe all the activities and relationships within a company? Obviously not. Think of the buzzing confusion of a customer service office or the zigs and zags of new product development. And what of airports and trading floors? These, we would suggest, are better depicted in different ways—as hubs and webs.

Hubs first. A *hub* serves as a coordinating center. It is any physical or conceptual point at which people, things, or information move. A building can be a hub—think of a school or an airport. So can a machine—a computer, for example. A manager can be a hub. Just think of a football coach. And so can a core competence, such as optics at Canon or bonding and coating at 3M. In fact, places that we usually consider chains may also be considered hubs. Draw a big circle around a factory, including its assembly line (a chain), and the whole place looks like a hub, to which parts and people flow and from which products emerge.

Hubs depict movement to and from one focal point. But oftentimes connections are more complicated than that. That's where *webs* come in. We are constantly being reminded that we live in the age of the network, where different "nodes"—be they people, teams, computers, or whatever else—connect in all kinds of ways. Webs, as we have come to see, are grids with no center; they allow open-ended communication and continuous movement of people and ideas.

Take new product development, for example. In the midst of a launch, the cast of characters talking to one another—often in very circuitous ways—will include managers, engineers, salespeople, and customers. Any complex project these days can be seen as a web. Think of how the Olympic Games are organized or how a movie is made. Everyone talks to everyone else, often with creative and unexpected outcomes.

The new vocabulary of organigraphs can expand how we view our organizations; it can even expand our thinking about strategic direction. Consider the exhibit "Organigraphs of a Canadian Bank." For years, the company had been a classic "silo" organization, with its businesses, such as insurance and brokerage, approaching customers independently. Then, as information sharing and cross-selling became competitive necessities, the bank began exploring other ways of organizing. One was to assign company representatives—personal financial advisers—to deal with customers for all the businesses, so as to present an integrated front. These advisers become, in effect, a hub for the customer. Another option was to place representatives from the different businesses in adjacent offices so that they could work cooperatively in dealing with customers—passing on leads and so forth. That way, the business representatives could work as a team—a web—while doing business with customers. Such options would have been available to the bank without organigraphs, of course, but the new vocabulary, and associated pictures, brought the choices into high relief.

Given the propensity of hubs and webs in organizations today, where does that leave the traditional organizational chart? The organizational chart treats everyone and everything as an independent box. And every one of those boxes is connected by a vertical chain—that is, a chain of authority. If that is how we see organizations, is it any wonder there has been so much restructuring and delayering, so much merging and outsourcing? These changes are initially driven by a reshuffling of boxes on paper—too often without consideration of an organization's real ways of doing business and creating value.

Organigraphs in Action

When you try to draw an organigraph using sets, chains, hubs, and webs, what happens? Almost anything. There is no right organigraph. Unlike the org chart with its strict rules of arrangement, an organigraph requires managers to create a customized picture of their company, something that involves imagination and an open mind. (Organigraphs can, in fact, include shapes besides sets, chains, hubs, and webs—as long as the shapes convey meaning. For instance, some organigraphs include funnels, suggesting a chain in which a transformation takes place.) Organigraphs can be disconcerting to those accustomed to doing things the traditional way. One manager we worked with resisted them initially, saying,

Organigraphs of a Canadian Bank

This organigraph depicts the bank's original structure. Each division operates as a silo—a member of a set—and approaches the customer independently.

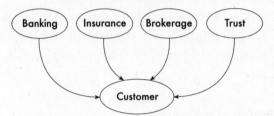

A second organigraph depicts one strategic option. All divisions converge on financial advisers—acting as a hub—who can approach each customer in an integrated way.

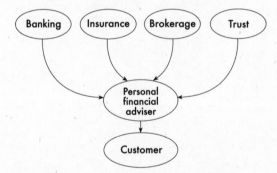

A third organigraph illuminates another strategic option. Representatives from each business work cooperatively—as a web—at each branch, but approach customers independently.

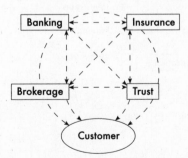

"But I like org charts. When something goes wrong in my company, I know exactly whom to call to fix it." Always formal authority! To draw an organigraph, you must accept the fact that it has less to do with names and titles than with relationships and processes.

To see how an organigraph works, let's look at the exhibit "Organigraph of a Newspaper." A newspaper brings in a variety of materials from society—news, pho-

Organigraph of a Newspaper

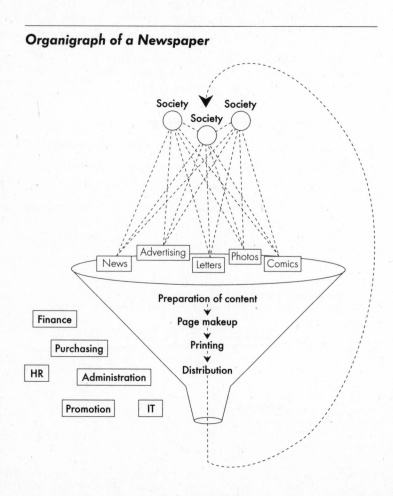

tographs, and the like. Employees at the newspaper screen the material, transform it, and assemble it into a single document. The document then goes to a plant for reproduction, and the copies are distributed back to society, indeed to many of the same people responsible for the inputs, such as letters to the editor and classified ads.

The newspaper organigraph shows that while the organization's overall flow is a chain, other forms coexist within it. The reporters' relationships with the community, for example, can be seen as a web: the stock-in-trade of many reporters is to build networks of sources. And the whole newspaper might be considered a hub, upon which all sorts of inputs converge—classified and other advertisements, letters to the editor, article ideas, and so on—to be dispersed back into society. Because they are not integral to the main linear flow of the organization, various support and administrative functions, such as purchasing and finance, are shown around the hub, not within it.

What a different picture than the traditional org chart! (For a comparison, see the exhibit "Newspaper Org Chart.") Those little stacked boxes imply an organization

Newspaper Org Chart

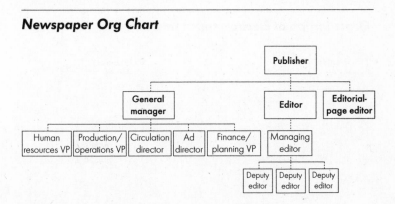

consisting of independent agents. The picture doesn't even show advertisers, and it suggests that the human resources department is somehow in the thick of the company's operating processes. The organigraph, in contrast, shows that advertisers are both sources of content (as part of the web) and customers and puts HR's role in perspective. It also draws attention to the scope of the business, suggesting which activities ought to be retained inside the core of the company and which might be candidates for outsourcing, such as printing and distribution.

The exhibit "Organigraph of Electrocomponents," showing a British distributor of electrical and mechanical items, depicts an entirely different business than that of the newspaper. When you actually visit the company, it *appears* to function like a web: an automatic machine picks a variety of different items from all over large warehouses and moves them to packing. But this activity is, in fact, more like a set of chains: each order is picked in careful sequence.

Overall, the company's work is a chain. Electrocomponents procures thousands of items, which are held in

Organigraph of Electrocomponents

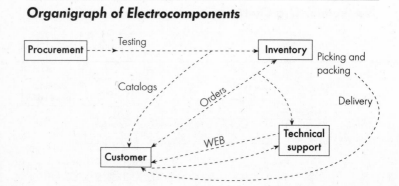

inventory. When customers place orders, products are picked off the shelves and delivered on a day's notice. But as is often the case, the company actually combines organizational forms. For example, the company's relationships with customers can also be seen as a web. Several times a year, Electrocomponents sends out catalogs to its customers, most of whom are engineers. They phone in their orders and can use the same call to ask for advice from the technical support staff, who are also engineers.

The organigraph we developed with Electrocomponents allowed managers to see nearly a dozen new opportunities to expand the business. "The picture forced us to think about what our real expertise was," recalls CEO Bob Lawson. "And we decided that it was in business-to-business relationships, not with consumers." As a result of that insight, Electrocomponents decided to expand significantly in Asia and to increase its Internet business. Further, the organigraph helped the company's managers see the strategic logic of segmenting its catalog. Having sent out only one version before, it now issues six specialized versions. The organigraph also showed managers opportunities to expand and sell the company's testing services. "At a glance, that diagram allowed us to see all sorts of new possibilities," Lawson says.

A Nest of Organizational Forms

Chains, hubs, webs, and sets can be found throughout most organizations. In the exhibit "Organigraph of Médecins Sans Frontières" (Doctors Without Borders), we take that concept one step further, depicting the nesting of such relationships—hubs within hubs within sets.

The organigraph shows a nonprofit that establishes emergency hospitals in disaster areas. Médecins Sans Frontières is made up of a set of national offices. There is no world headquarters—no hub. Rather, CEOs from the national office meet periodically, and when a crisis arises, people from the offices communicate informally. They form a loose web.

Each national office is, however, a hub unto itself. (See the largest circle in the exhibit.) The office is the focal point for the collection of professionals, supplies, funds, and procedures. Each office, for instance, holds its own donations in the bank and has a list of physicians prepared to go on assignment. When a crisis occurs, a national office assembles resources—people, supplies, and money. It then ships them to the troubled area. There, a hospital is created—a temporary organization—itself a hub to which the ill are brought. Each patient also becomes a hub in his or her own

Organigraph of Médecins Sans Frontières

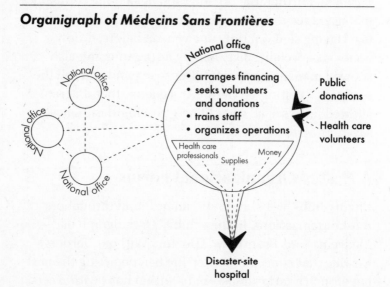

right, on the receiving end of various health care professionals, medicines, and food.

The organigraph shows that there are four distinct
areas of operation within this nonprofit:

- a national office coordinates resources available for
  relief operations;

- that office also assembles those resources at the time
  of a particular relief operation;

- chain transfers the relief resources from the national
  office to the hospital site;

- that hospital then delivers health care.

The organigraph makes clear the managerial realities
the nonprofit faces. For example, one can see from the
illustration that the burden of promoting the organization and raising money for it lies on the national offices
themselves. The loose web that serves as an umbrella for
the set of national offices is not organized to do so. Further, the organigraph shows operating autonomy on
site—yet simultaneously illuminates the need to facilitate information flow between the national office and the
disaster area.

Competencies as Hubs

Earlier we described a conglomerate as a set of loosely
coupled businesses. That certainly makes sense for
highly diversified operations, especially ones that have
grown through the acquisition of businesses in unrelated
industries. The divisions constitute a portfolio, held
together by a headquarters that manages the flow of capital and imposes financial standards of performance.

But these days, the notion of conglomeration has given way to the concept of core competence: that the many products of companies such as Canon or 3M—which have grown more by the internal development of new products than by the acquisition of external businesses— are held together by some core of knowledge, skills, or resources. These competencies, then, can be seen as the *hub* of the organization, to which all activities relate.

Consider the exhibit "Organigraph of Frontec," which shows a Canadian company with about $125 million in annual sales. Founded in 1986, Frontec's first business was providing staff and supplies to the military's early warning stations in the far north. From there, it branched into other activities, such as construction, the running of hotels and airports, and a contract for the installation of communications equipment on military

Organigraph of Frontec

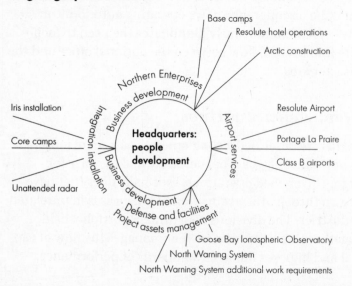

vehicles—mostly in remote, dangerous locations, often with challenging logistics. Frontec employees have worked with polar bears nearby—one operation is 400 miles from the North Pole—and sometimes have to fly helicopters in whiteouts. Such conditions explain why a primary core competence of the company is people development. The most important job for senior managers is to ensure that the right people are in charge of field operations. They do so by carefully selecting and developing key personnel.

A second core competence is business development, shown in the organigraph as closer to the field operations. The various ventures are listed all around the business development competence, as satellites, or quasi-independent business activities, which are shown to be associated with various categories such as Airport Services and Northern Enterprises.

The organigraph helped Frontec's senior managers communicate their self-image of a "frontier venturer" to a board of directors that was accustomed to more conventional organizations. It allowed managers to illustrate the company's character—that it is a company organized around competencies that allow it to venture into new and daring businesses in uncharted locations.

Putting Management in Its Place

One of the greatest benefits of seeing organizations differently is that we begin to see management differently. Isn't it about time? In the traditional organizational chart, senior managers always appear on top. But is that always the best place for them?

We think not. The very notion of "top management" may long have had a debilitating effect on organizations and on the behaviors of managers themselves. Bear in mind that "top management" is just a metaphor. In reality, the top manager is on top of nothing but a chart. Managers who see themselves on top of their organizations may not really be on top of what takes place there. They may simply be too distant from the actual work being done.

Each organizational form suggests a different philosophy of managing. Sets suggest that managers stay away from the action, watching and comparing. In a conglomerate, for example, executives at headquarters oversee the divisions for the purposes of allocation. Their job, basically, is to decide who gets what resources.

The chain puts a boss above as well, but in this case above each link—a manager for each and a manager for all. In other words, the chain of command is laid over the chain of operations. The chain of operations is clear and orderly, and the chain of management exists primarily to keep it that way—for control.

It is when we move on to hubs and webs that management moves off its pedestal. In the hub, management appears in the center, around which activities revolve, as can be seen in the organigraphs of Médecins Sans Frontières and Frontec. Management at the center has an interesting implication: whoever is at the center *becomes* the manager. For example, if the hospital patient is a hub, then the nurse—not the doctor, not the chief of staff—is the manager. Why? Because the nurse coordinates the array of services that converge on the patient. In a real sense, nursing is managing—which means that managing can extend beyond formal authority.

Managing at the center implies something profoundly different from managing on top. While the chain controls, the hub coordinates. The chain may pretend to empower; the hub brings together people who are intrinsically empowered. As suggested in Frontec's organigraph, the center holds the whole together by reinforcing the organization's competencies at its core.

And where can we find management in the web? At first glance, the answer is not clear. A more careful look, however, suggests that good management acts throughout the web. In a network—a project or an alliance, for example—managers have to be *everywhere*. In practical terms, that means out from behind their desks—in design studios, in airplanes on the way to offices and clients, and in other places where real work happens. Management that is not everywhere in the web is nowhere. The web is so fluid that managers cannot afford to remain in the center. In the web, managers have to move around, literally as well as figuratively, in order to facilitate collaboration and energize the whole network. They need to encourage people who already know how to do their work and do it well.

In a web, management can also be *everyone*. Whoever draws things together becomes a de facto manager. All kinds of people are managers who do not carry that official title, be it scientists in a research lab or salespeople in the field. (For an illustration of this point, see the exhibit "The Four Philosophies of Managing.")

In one sense, these philosophies of managing—allocating in the set, controlling in the chain, coordinating in the hub, and energizing in the web—are apt metaphors. Chains are heavy, webs are light. Hubs, in between, can explode or implode if not managed correctly. Follow a chain and you know where you will end up. Just don't try to go anywhere else! Find a hub and you know where to begin or end. Not so for the set, which can start and end in different places. The web, by contrast, can take you

The Four Philosophies of Managing

In the set, managers look it over—they allocate.

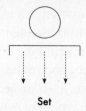

Set

In the chain, managers lay it on—they control.

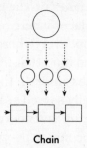

Chain

In the hub, managers draw it in—they coordinate.

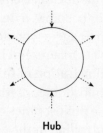

Hub

In the web, managers link it all—they energize.

Web

every which way. That can leave you flexible or flustered—and often both.

For companies to thrive in today's economy, management has to be put in its place—in another place, that is. Not atop the chart—at least not in all but the most tightly controlled, highly programmed bureaucracies—but down into its essence, whether at a center, as a hub, or throughout, as a web. That way those old charts can be put in their place, too (in something round that sits on the floor but is not a hub). By viewing management in this way, we can recognize it for what it has to be: the servant of the organization, not its purpose.

Do you see?

Originally published in September–October 1999
Reprint 99506

Stop Fighting Fires

ROGER BOHN

Executive Summary

FIRE FIGHTING is an old, familiar way of doing business, especially when developing new products and ramping up manufacturing. But fire fighting consumes an organization's resources and damages productivity. People rush from task to task, rarely completing one job before being interrupted by another. And serious problem solving degenerates into quick-and-dirty patching. Managers must perform a juggling act, deciding where to allocate overworked people and which crises to ignore for the moment.

What factors underly this destructive pattern? Fire fighting isn't an irrational response to high-pressure management situations. Rather, it derives from what seems like a reasonable set of rules—investigate all problems, for example, or assign the most difficult problems to your best troubleshooter. Ultimately, however, fire-fighting organizations fail to solve problems adequately and forgo so many opportunities that overall performance plummets.

Some companies never fight fires, even though they have just as much work and just as many resource constraints as other companies do. They have strong problem-solving cultures. They perform triage. They set realistic deadlines. They don't tackle a problem unless they're committed to understanding its root cause and finding a valid solution. And they don't reward fire-fighting behavior.

Transforming a fire-fighting organization into a problem-solving one is not easy. But there are tactical, strategic, and cultural methods for pulling your company out of fire-fighting mode.

IN BUSINESS ORGANIZATIONS, there are invariably more problems than people have the time to deal with. At best, this leads to situations where minor problems are ignored. At worst, chronic fire fighting consumes an operation's resources. Companies with complex R&D and manufacturing processes are particularly prone to destructive fire fighting. Managers and engineers rush from task to task, not completing one before another interrupts them. Serious problem-solving efforts degenerate into quick-and-dirty patching. Productivity suffers. Managing becomes a constant juggling act of deciding where to allocate overworked people and which incipient crisis to ignore for the moment.

For several years, my late colleague Ramchandran Jaikumar and I observed fire-fighting behavior in many manufacturing and new-product-development settings. When we described what we'd seen, people instantly recognized what we were talking about—indeed, most of them said they fought fires in their own professional lives all the time. Yet with a few exceptions, the fire-fighting syndrome has stayed off the radar screens of organizational theorists.[1] It deserves far more attention. In fact, fire fighting is one of the most serious problems facing many managers of complex, change-driven processes.

From our observations, fire fighting is best character-ized as a collection of symptoms. You're a victim if three of the following linked elements are chronic within your business unit or division.

- *There isn't enough time to solve all the problems.* There are more problems than the problem solvers—engi-neers, managers, or other knowledge workers—can deal with properly.

- *Solutions are incomplete.* Many problems are patched, not solved. That is, the superficial effects are dealt with, but the underlying causes are not fixed.

- *Problems recur and cascade.* Incomplete solutions cause old problems to reemerge or actually create new problems, sometimes elsewhere in the organization.

- *Urgency supersedes importance.* Ongoing problem-solving efforts and long-range activities, such as developing new processes, are repeatedly interrupted or deferred because fires must be extinguished.

- *Many problems become crises.* Problems smolder until they flare up, often just before a deadline. Then they require heroic efforts to solve.

- *Performance drops.* So many problems are solved inadequately and so many opportunities forgone that overall performance plummets.

The recent Mars Climate Orbiter crash is an example of the insidious nature of fire fighting. The crash was traced to a simple communication problem—one engineering group used metric units of measurement, another used English units—but that explanation masks a more complex underlying problem. According to a NASA report published shortly before the crash, the subcontractor staff early in the project was smaller than planned. This led to delays, work-arounds, and poor technical decisions, all of which required catch-up work later. Engineering staff was borrowed from other projects in their early phases—thus forcing those projects into the same position. Engineers worked 70-hour weeks to meet deadlines, causing more errors in the short run and declines in effectiveness in the long run. Early warning signs were missed or ignored. According to a report after the crash, the navigation error that caused the crash could probably have been corrected by a contingency burn, but a decision on whether to perform the burn was never made because of the crush of other urgent work. This is classic fire fighting.

Fire fighting isn't necessarily disastrous. Clearly it hampers performance, but there are worse alternatives. Rigid bureaucratic rules, for example, can help a company avoid fire fighting altogether, but at the price of almost no problems getting solved. Also, sometimes even a well-managed organization slips into fire-fighting mode temporarily without creating long-term problems. The danger is that the more intense fire fighting becomes, the more difficult it is to escape from.

There are some companies that never fight fires, even though they have just as much work and just as many resource constraints as companies that do. How do they avoid fire fighting? The short answer is that they have strong problem-solving cultures. They don't tackle a problem unless they're committed to understanding its root cause and finding a valid solution. They perform triage. They set realistic deadlines. Perhaps most important, they don't reward fire fighting.

A Simple Model of Fire Fighting

Before we can move on to what to do about fire fighting, we need to look more closely at its underlying causes. A simple model captures the essential issues. (See the exhibit "How Problems Flow Through Organizations.")

Let's assume that the organization is a factory engineering group, although it could easily be an R&D facility or a software development group. As problems arise—from customers' complaints, special orders, quality lapses, supplier difficulties, and other sources—they are sent into a queue until an engineer has time to work on them.

As engineers finish a problem, they report to a manager who presides over the queue, deciding which problems are the most urgent and who should solve each one. Solving a problem takes time: an engineer must study the symptoms, confirm that the problem is real, conduct

How Problems Flow Through Organizations

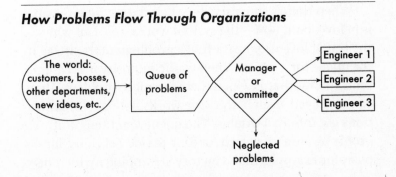

background research, diagnose its causes, search for a good solution, and implement the solution. Problems come in different shapes and sizes and hence require different amounts of time. Allocating the tasks is itself fairly complex. Each engineer works on several problems at once, and each is better at some problems than others. Engineers may function in teams, and the teams for each problem can differ. Vacations and routine tasks complicate scheduling. Each of these complexities reduces the attainable efficiency of the system and makes the manager's decisions harder.

When severe fire fighting sets in, managers and engineers find themselves spending more time responding to irate queries than working productively.

A key number in this system is the *traffic intensity*—the number of problems relative to the resources devoted to problem solving. Traffic intensity increases when there are more problems or when the problems take longer to solve. It decreases when more problem solvers are brought into the picture.

$$\text{Traffic intensity} = \frac{\left(\begin{array}{c}\text{Days} \\ \text{to solve}\end{array}\right) \times \left(\begin{array}{c}\text{Number of new} \\ \text{problems per day}\end{array}\right)}{\text{Number of engineers}}$$

When there's some slack—when the traffic intensity is below about 80%—the system works well. But when the traffic intensity nears 100%, problems start sitting in the queue for a while. When traffic intensity is greater than 100%—that is, when there are more problems than can be solved, even if everyone works flat out—organizations get into real trouble. The queue lengthens and problems aren't resolved for long periods of time. Suppose, for example, that a factory is ramping up for a new product, and roughly three significant problems crop up every day. Four engineers each take an average of two days per problem, so every day the queue of unsolved problems grows by one. By the end of the third week, 15 problems are waiting for attention.

As the queue grows, the engineers and their managers experience various pressures—the self-imposed pressure of knowing they're behind, pressure from customers who want the product immediately, pressure from senior managers who are upset by customers' complaints. This is when severe fire fighting can set in. Managers and engineers let some problems jump the queue for political reasons. They drop problem A (a machine that keeps breaking down, causing bottlenecks) to find a solution for problem B (a serious quality defect) because B reaches crisis proportions. They put lots of effort into problem C (implementing manufacturing changes for a new set of product enhancements), only to find that the enhancements are indefinitely postponed because they did not work in beta testing. And they find themselves spending more time responding to irate inquiries than working productively. (See the table "Rational Rules, Irrational Results" for more detail about the seemingly reasonable organizational responses to overlong work queues.)

In other words, work becomes far less efficient precisely when the most work needs to get done. The longer the backlog, the more things bog down. Engineers start spending time away from normal work—they're stuck in meetings to set priorities about which fire to fight next; they're handling special rush jobs for customers whose orders have been delayed; they're solving problems that later get "overtaken by events." In general, they're dealing with the chaos and information overload that ensue

Rational Rules, Irrational Results

Organizations have developed many rules of thumb for problem solving.
And indeed, when a company is not under stress, these rules may be
good ones. They can also be helpful for knowledge workers who are
developing their individual reputations. But when an organization is in
fire-fighting mode, these rules are pernicious.

	Rule of Thumb	But Think Again
Selecting Problems	Investigate every apparent problem.	If you don't set priorities, important problems don't get solved. Push minutiae off the to-do list.
	Work on all the things you are asked to work on.	If you allow people outside your group to set your agenda, you'll never stay on top of things.
	Always work on the problem with the nearest deadline.	If you always work on the deliverable that's due soonest, everything else gets delayed and eventually becomes a crisis, too.
	Behave as if the urgency of the task is proportional to the rank of the person requesting it.	Sometimes it is, sometimes it's not.
Solving Problems	Be sure that everyone who might be affected or able to help comes to meetings. Consult and inform widely before acting.	All those well-intentioned meetings eat away at problem-solving time.
	Give people short deadlines—they'll work harder. If they make the deadlines, you probably gave them too much time.	It's true that most motivated people work harder under pressure (until they burn out), but they are also forced to cut corners.
	If you can't solve a problem completely, do the best you can. If you are too busy to fix something properly, do as much as possible.	This rule quickly leads to patching.
	Give all difficult problems to your best troubleshooter.	That person gets overwhelmed, and others don't gain experience.
	Give your trusted people complete discretion about how they solve problems. Even junior engineers know how to solve problems; don't waste their time with nontechnical training.	You can't create a problem-solving culture if you don't train problem solvers.

when fire fighting is rampant. But that's not the worst of it.

Counterproductive Problem Solving

The really bad news is that under fire-fighting conditions, pressures push engineers to solve problems not just inefficiently but badly. They don't work on a problem long enough to uncover its root cause—they just make a gut-feel diagnosis. Then, instead of testing their hypothetical diagnosis offline, they introduce a hasty change in the process. And if the quick fix doesn't solve the problem completely (it is usually unclear whether it helped or not), they leave it in place and try another solution. They don't solve the problem because they don't take the time to approach it systematically.

At best, this superficial problem solving, or patching, takes more time than systematic problem solving. Consider the following example: A manufacturer of steel cords had hundreds of machines in one facility. Because machine uptime was important, the company encouraged maintenance engineers to respond to breakdowns as quickly as possible. Even so, overall performance didn't improve. Only after the company started keeping and analyzing records machine by machine instead of person by person did it realize that engineers were constantly interrupted while repairing one machine because another had failed. They would make a quick fix and move on to the next machine. Each original machine breakdown, as it turned out, generated many visits; on average, a problem was patched three times before it was finally solved.

Patching not only takes more time than systematic problem solving, it also fails to fix problems. A longer story shows why. A colleague and I recently helped an electronics company solve a major yield problem. The company fabricated parts in one U.S. factory and assembled them in another. The company had transferred assembly to Asia to reduce labor costs just as a new product was being introduced. At about this time, the assembly yields crashed; half or more of the devices failed. Customers were pleading for more product, but the company couldn't meet demand. The result was an outbreak of fire fighting. A team was charged with finding a quick solution. Each member had a pet theory about what was happening and how changing the process would fix it. The Asian factory dutifully implemented one trial "solution" after another. Because of constraints at the factory, it took about a month to get the results from each trial.

Although this went on for months, the team got no closer to understanding the problem's cause. Because team members didn't think they had time, they never ran a controlled trial in which the same batch was assembled in both Asia and the United States. Hence there was no proof that the problem was due to a difference between the two facilities; it could have resulted from a change in fabrication that happened to coincide with the factory move. After all, the fabrication process was ramping up at the same time. Ironically, the company's senior management talked a lot about using modern quality methods and systematic problem solving. But once the pressure from customers got too great, people fell back on patching, believing it would deliver faster results.

We suggested that the company develop a scientific understanding of the problem. To that end, we used lab experiments, mathematical analysis, and large controlled experiments in the factory. The main problem turned out to be a previously unknown temperature sensitivity in assembly, the direct result of a process change that had been instituted to solve a problem the year before. It had been happening in both

Haphazardly introduced changes can easily create new problems elsewhere in the process.

the U.S. and Asian plants, but seemingly inconsequential differences between them made the situation much worse in Asia. Once the cause of the problem was understood, fixing it was straightforward. Based on its new knowledge, the company also improved yields on many other products. And the knowledge gave the company a significant advantage over competitors grappling with similar problems. It took months to solve the problem this way, but fire fighting had taken even longer, to no avail.

When changes are introduced haphazardly, as they were for this process, they are frequently institutionalized without careful study. For example, noted author Primo Levi worked briefly after World War II as a chemist in a paint factory. Many years later, he met an old friend who was still working there. The friend told him the factory was producing an anticorrosion paint that contained a compound likely to accelerate corrosion. When the friend had questioned his bosses, he was told that the paint had always been made that way, that the compound was absolutely necessary, and that he shouldn't change anything. As it happened, Levi had first included the compound in the formula. He did it strictly as a temporary measure to counter contamination in an important raw material, but his rationale was forgotten when he left, and the recipe was carved in stone.

Haphazardly introduced changes raise an even more serious issue: they can easily create new problems elsewhere in the process. That happens all the time in software development: while patching one bug, you create another. The same thing often happens in factories. In a metal-working factory, in order to improve performance of their part of the process, engineers changed the makeup of a coating. Months later, the company's biggest customer developed a major problem: a metal framework that needed to be affixed to a rubber part no longer stuck to that part. The problem, stemming from the change in the coating, turned out to be extremely expensive for both the customer and the company—all the more so, of course, because the cause didn't become clear for a long time. Patching can create new problems whenever the patches are not validated carefully.

Patching can be justified in a few situations. For example, in software development it's common to add code that checks for a particular error. If that error occurs, the software delivers an error message and stops further computation. This is a patch because it does not solve the real problem, but it does prevent it from worsening. And in manufacturing, it's common to add another inspection step when an as-yet-unresolved problem exists so flawed products can be pulled. This weeding out raises costs, but it avoids passing on the defective parts. Such superficial solutions are acceptable if several conditions are met. First, the patches should ameliorate much of the damage even though they don't address the cause. Second, they should be solid enough that they won't break down later. And third, they should have a better benefit-cost ratio than other solutions. The key cost here is not dollars but engineering time.

With those exceptions, patching is destructive. Solution rates fall and the number of hidden problems rises. (See the exhibit "The Effects of Fire-Fighting Syndrome.") The new problems that patching has created, and the old ones that it has failed to solve, act up more and more, until a large fraction of the incoming problems are actually old ones returning. The engineer's environment becomes increasingly chaotic, which makes it harder to run experiments and pin down problems. In some cases, the organization's ability to solve problems collapses completely, and overall performance plummets.[2] At that point, senior management may need to take drastic action—like outsourcing much of the work, shutting down and starting over, or bringing in a massive infusion of outside help. Such turnarounds are a major drain on money and management time. And even when executives intervene, they sometimes make fire fighting worse by tackling only the current crisis without fixing its deeper causes. Fortunately, there are ways to avoid reaching such a crisis point.

The Effects of Fire-Fighting Syndrome

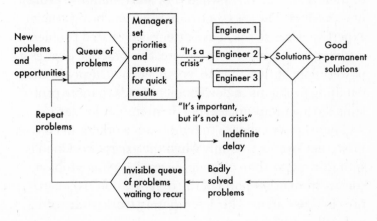

You Can Prevent Fires

There are several ways to eliminate fire fighting. They can be loosely sorted into three categories: tactical, strategic, and cultural.

TACTICAL METHODS

Tactical methods can be put into effect quickly without making high-level policy changes. Although some of the methods are culturally difficult in U.S. companies, many are simple to apply once a company recognizes the dangers of fire fighting.

Add temporary problem solvers. When the rate of new problems jumps, bringing in temporary assistance is a good short-term solution. Fire-fighting departments, the real kind, put out calls for firefighters from neighboring areas to deal with the biggest blazes. In high tech, most hard-disk-drive companies have learned to send development engineers from the United States directly to their Asian factories when they start manufacturing a new product. These extra troubleshooters bring crucial expertise because they have often seen related problems during prototyping. Furthermore, this practice creates a powerful incentive: the U.S. engineers quickly learn that patching problems in development leads to more problems during ramp-up, leaving them in Asia longer.

There are drawbacks to temporary workers, of course. First, they're effective only when the excess workload is sporadic rather than chronic. Second, pulling problem solvers from other parts of the organization risks setting fires in those areas. Third, temporary workers are often unfamiliar with the situation.

Shut down operations. It's been said before, but an ounce of prevention is worth a pound of cure. When the number of problems becomes too large, shut down operations until all are solved. Or, allow a new problem into the queue only when an old one is removed. Organizations where fire fighting is not part of the culture do this instinctively during product ramp-up. Some Hewlett-Packard development centers shut down a pilot line for the rest of the day once a certain number of problems is backlogged because until those problems are solved, there is no stable baseline for detecting and solving additional problems. Few companies have the fortitude to limit the queue size during normal operations.

Perform triage. Another approach to limiting the queue is to do deliberately what will happen anyway: admit that some problems will not be solved. The triage technique, borrowed from military medicine, controls the queue by regulating entry. Rather than let problems queue up indefinitely, or work their way through the queue only to be worked on sporadically, decide whether to commit resources to a problem when it first arises. This technique is organizationally difficult. It is much easier to tell people, "We'll get to your problem as soon as we can," and delegate it to someone who is overworked, than to say, "We've decided your problem isn't critical so we're not going to fix it."

STRATEGIC METHODS

Strategic approaches to fire fighting take longer to implement than tactical methods, but they pay off across a range of projects and over long periods. Even if they don't eliminate fire fighting completely, they increase the number of problems solved. The first several changes we mention focus on product design, but they have a major impact on manufacturing as well.

Change design strategies.   New product design has come a long way in the past decade. In some industries, companies have increased the commonality of designs across generations and products. That has reduced the number of design problems within and across product generations as well as the changes, and therefore the problems, in manufacturing. Commonality can be further enhanced by modular designs, which allow improvement of one section of a product without much change to others.

For example, hard-disk-drive companies used to have separate teams on successive drive generations—leading to designs where even the screws changed with each product. But gradually they adopted the "platform" concept. Now the capacity of a drive can be doubled by changing only the heads, media, and firmware, and substituting the latest and fastest signal processing chips on the circuit card. The new design is manufactured almost exactly as the previous one was, and the problems are concentrated in the new areas. Seagate, for instance, can transfer some products into manufacturing by moving only a few development engineers to the factory temporarily; five years ago, 20 or more were commonly needed.

Outsource some parts of design.   Companies in the auto industry have moved toward "black box" design: they specify only the characteristics of a subsystem, including its size, weight, power requirements, and performance. The subcontractor building the subsystem determines the best way to achieve the objectives, including which technologies to use. While the total number of problems may not go down, many are removed from the central design team.

Solve classes of problems, not individual problems. It's sometimes possible to group seemingly diverse problems together, determine a set of underlying causes, and then learn about those causes. Once they are understood, solving the individual problems is often straightforward.

An example of problem classes comes from the semiconductor industry. When integrated circuits were first manufactured, most circuits had to be thrown away because of defects. Companies developed codes for describing the failures based on which tests the circuits failed. When losses due to a particular code were high, a team would try to figure out why. Gradually it became clear that

Determining classes of problems requires a deliberate, extensive, and sustained commitment to formal problem solving —exactly what fire fighting pushes out.

many individual problems were caused by particles falling on wafer surfaces and ruining the circuits. "Particle-caused defects" was thus a problem class. It shifted engineers' attention from various specific failure codes to one well-defined problem: learning where the particles came from and how to get rid of them.

Eventually companies redesigned manufacturing facilities, turning them into "clean rooms" where air filters remove particles. As circuits got smaller, ever smaller particles became problematic. Another breakthrough came when engineers realized that people brought particles into the clean rooms. Again, this was a problem class: "contamination from people." The companies solved many contamination problems at once by requiring workers to dress in special garments and forbidding the use of makeup and other skin coatings.

Determining classes of problems requires a deliberate, extensive, and sustained commitment to formal problem solving. A company must correlate information from different parts of the organization over long periods of time, develop scientific models that yield higher levels of process understanding, and run controlled experimentation in the factory. These are exactly the kinds of long-term activities that fire fighting pushes out.

Use learning lines. Learning lines are production lines run to maximize real problem solving. Unlike pilot lines, which use special equipment and operators, learning lines use standard materials to make real products for customers. Thus they're exposed to all the vicissitudes of the rest of the factory, such as bad material batches, unreliable machines, and careless operators. They're used to gather data, run diagnostic experiments, debug processes, and do intensive problem solving, especially during manufacturing ramp-up. Often the performance of learning lines is the best in the factory, because innovations are put in place there first and problems are rapidly detected and solved. Part of the art of using a learning line is ensuring that it faithfully reflects conditions throughout the factory—and that improvements are quickly transferred to the rest of the plant. This is accomplished by not isolating engineers on the learning line. Every engineer should be able to use the learning line as a laboratory for investigation.

Develop more problem solvers. One of the successes of the TQM movement is that nonengineers have been trained to solve simple problems. Even though they are not as fast or as knowledgeable as engineers, technicians and others can free up resources for difficult problems by handling many of the more mundane ones.

CULTURAL METHODS

Cultural changes require shifts in the mind-set of the whole organization and in the behavior of senior managers. Extra work in organizations—even those that don't usually fight fires—will occasionally create pressure to begin fire fighting. At these times, the organization's problem-solving culture is critical. If managers are too far removed from the problems to see the consequences, and if the reward system favors firefighters, then the vicious cycle of fire fighting will begin. Avoiding this depends on the culture of middle and senior managers. We suggest the following guidelines.

Don't tolerate patching. The importance of this point has already been discussed, but enforcing it requires support at all levels of management. At Intel, for example, managers from the CEO on down have extensive line problem-solving experience and can distinguish a patch from a real solution. If subordinates find that hasty solutions come back and bite them, organizationally speaking, they will avoid patching.

In most U.S. organizations, the hero is the one who puts out the biggest fires. But where were these heroes when the problems started?

Don't push to meet deadlines at all costs. Such goals always favor fire fighting. Instead, be flexible about deadlines. Measure development projects by the number of outstanding problems. Most companies measure "open issues" and problems discovered after product release, and many good factories have accurate lists and measures of unsolved problems. If this list stays the same or grows for more than a month after a product introduction, the organization is in fire-fighting mode.

Don't reward fire fighting. In most U.S. organizations, the hero is the one who puts out the biggest fires. But where were these heroes when the problems started? Why didn't they intervene sooner, before the problems grew so big? Companies should reward managers who don't have a lot of fires to put out and who practice long-term prevention and systematic problem solving.

Building a Problem-Solving Organization

In today's highly dynamic business environments, the key tasks for people in charge are innovating, improving, and dealing with the unexpected. The "unexpected" takes the form of problems whose solutions can open the door to innovation and improvement. Seen in this light, managers have a lot in common with engineers—and they're just as prone to fire fighting.

So how does a fire-fighting organization transform itself into a problem-solving organization? It must recognize that the self-perpetuating fire-fighting syndrome is not an inherently irrational response to high-pressure management situations. Its genesis, rather, is a set of rules and behaviors that seem reasonable but really cause fire fighting in the long run. An organization must not only abandon these seemingly logical practices but also adopt techniques that, at first blush, appear irrational.

Curing the fire-fighting syndrome is not easy. Established organizational culture and short-sighted logic often work against it. Management that believes people work harder under pressure exacerbates the condition. But pulling your company out of fire-fighting mode is worth the effort because fire fighting drains your best workers; no matter how hard they work, they can't put all the fires out. The obvious, albeit extreme, risk of fire fighting is that the organization will have to withdraw a product line or shut down a plant that has been rendered ineffectual. The less obvious but just as important risk is that the organization's best problem solvers will become fed up and leave. Building a problem-solving organization is difficult, but the benefits are clear and the choice unambiguous.

Computer Thrashing

A COMPUTER OPERATING SYSTEM (OS) can exhibit a behavior that is analogous to fire fighting. An OS has many demands placed on it simultaneously. For example, desktop PCs monitor a network connection, update the clock, interpret keystrokes, update the display, perform calculations, drive a printer, accept data from the hard-disk drive, collect garbage, and so forth. PC operating systems now also let end users run several programs at once: playing a music CD, downloading e-mail, and typing on a word processor, for example. Yet almost all computers have only one central processor, which switches among the various activities so that they appear to be going on simultaneously. Of course, sometimes the computer has more work than it can handle immediately—the traffic intensity is greater than 100%. The user experiences this as a slowdown, such as a stutter in the music or a pause in the screen update.

For a computer to work effectively, the OS must follow rules for switching among tasks on the basis of priorities. Handling communications inputs, for instance, is more urgent than most other jobs. But each "switch" itself consumes CPU time, much like the reduction in problem-solving effectiveness that occurs when engineers divide their attention between problems. Systems designers learned early that without well-defined rules governing task switching, an OS can become consumed with it—a phenomenon known as thrashing.

One insight from the OS analogy is that no fixed set of priority rules is effective under all circumstances. If, for example, an OS must process many short jobs and a few very long ones, priorities should be set to ensure that long jobs are allotted more time than short ones. But if all are long jobs, assigning equal time slices to each will result in none getting completed for a very long time. In that case, priorities should be set to ensure that some jobs are completed before time is allocated to the others. Managing fire fighting, like setting priorities in OSs, will not happen if you follow simple, rigid rules.

Notes

1. Robert Hayes is one of the exceptions, although he didn't use our term for it. In 1981, he hypothesized that one reason American factories were more chaotic than Japanese factories was a difference in culture. He wrote: "American managers actually *enjoy* crises; they often get their greatest personal satisfaction, the most recognition, and their

biggest rewards from solving crises. Crises are part of what makes work fun. To Japanese managers, however, a crisis is evidence of failure." ("Why Japanese Factories Work," HBR July–August 1981).

2. In "Beating Murphy's Law," which I coauthored with Dorothy Leonard-Barton and W. Bruce Chew (*Sloan Management Review*, Spring 1991), we discuss a case where a factory's entire production came to a halt, partly as a result of cascading fire fighting.

Originally published in July–August 2000
Reprint R00402

About the Contributors

CHRIS ARGYRIS is the James Conant Professor Emeritus of Education and Organizational Behavior at Harvard University. He has consulted to numerous private and governmental organizations. He has received many awards including eleven honorary degrees and Lifetime Contribution Awards from the Academy of Management, American Psychological Association, and American Society of Training Directors. His most recent books are *Flawed Advice* and *On Organizational Learning*. He is currently Director of Monitor Group.

ROGER BOHN is Associate Professor at the University of California, San Diego, where he teaches technology and operations management. His main area of research centers on speeding up the development of technology by engineers. He has also been involved in electricity deregulation in California, an extreme case of fire fighting by politicians and an entire industry. He can be reached by e-mail at Roger_bohn@alum.mit.edu.

JOHN SEELY BROWN is the former Director of the Xerox Palo Alto Research Center (PARC) and is currently the Chief Innovation Officer of the recently formed company, 12 Entrepreneuring. Over the years, his research has focused on human learning and the management of radical innovation. His additional research interests include digital culture, ubiquitous computing, user-centering design, and organizational learning. Brown is a cofounder of the Institute for Research on Learning, a member of the National Academy of Education, and a Fellow of the American Association for Artificial Intelligence. He also serves on numerous boards of directors and advisory boards. Among his awards are the 1998 Industrial Research Institute Medal for outstanding accomplishments in technological innovation, the 1999 Holland Award in recognition of the best paper published in Research Technology Management in 1998, and a bronze medal for the film *Art • Lunch • Internet • Dinner* of which he was an executive producer. He has published over a hundred papers in scientific journals and has edited or coauthored the books *Seeing Differently: Insights on Innovation* and *The Social Life of Information.*

PAUL DUGUID is a historian and social theorist affiliated with the University of California, Berkeley, and the Xerox Palo Alto Research Center. He was formally a member of the Institute for Research on Learning in Palo Alto. His interest in multidisciplinary, collaborative research has led him to work with social scientists, computer scientists, economists, linguists, management theorists, and social psychologists. While continuing to address the issues reflected in his book, *The Social Life of Information,* coauthored with John Seely Brown, he is also investigating the historical development of the institutions that shaped international trade in the eighteenth century. His writing has appeared in a broad array of scholarly fields and journals including anthropology, business and business history, cognitive science, computer science, design, education, economic history, human-computer interaction, management, organization theory, and wine history. Duguid has also written essays and reviews for a variety of less specialized publications, including the *Times Literary Supplement, The Nation,* and the *Threepenny Review.*

KATHLEEN M. EISENHARDT is Professor of Strategy and Organization at the School of Engineering, Stanford University, and Research Director of the Stanford Technology Ventures Program. Her research and teaching focus on managing in high-velocity, intensely competitive markets. Her awards include the Pacific Telesis Foundation for her ideas on fast strategic decision making, the Whittemore Prize for her writing on organizing global firms in rapidly changing markets, and the George R. Terry Book Award for her book, *Competing on the Edge: Strategy as Structured Chaos*, coauthored with Shona L. Brown.

D. CHARLES GALUNIC is Associate Professor and Area Coordinator of Organizational Behavior at INSEAD. His research examines organizational innovation, change, and learning. A former Rhodes Scholar, his awards include the Louis Pondy Award from the Academy of Management. The author of numerous articles, his publications have appeared in the *Academy of Management Journal*, *Strategic Management Journal*, *Organization Science*, *Research in Organizational Behavior*, and *Harvard Business Review*. He is also on the editorial review board of *Organization Science* and *The Strategic Management Journal*, and is a 1998 convenor for the European Group for Organization Studies.

MORTEN T. HANSEN is on leave as Assistant Professor in Business Administration at Harvard Business School and is currently Manager in the San Francisco office of the Boston Consulting Group. He has spent a number of years researching effective knowledge sharing in large companies and is an expert on knowledge management. His research has appeared not only in *Harvard Business Review*, but also in academic publications such as *Administrative Science Quarterly* and *Strategic Management Journal*, and in a number of media articles in the *New York Times*, *Business Week*, and the *Wall*

Street Journal. While at Harvard, he taught an MBA course that covered the topics of organizational learning and knowledge management.

HENRY MINTZBERG is Cleghorn Professor of Management Studies at McGill University in Montreal, Canada, and Visiting Scholar at INSEAD in Fontainebleau, France. His research has dealt with issues of general management and organizations, focusing on the nature of managerial work, forms of organizing, and the strategy formation process. Prior to his career in academia, he worked in operational research for the Canadian National Railways. He is the author of ten books, including *The Nature of Managerial Work*, *The Structuring of Organizations*, *Mintzberg on Management*, *The Rise and Fall of Strategic Planning*, *The Canadian Condition*, and *Strategy Safari*, and has won The McKinsey Prize for two of his *Harvard Business Review* articles. He was recently named an Officer of the Order of Canada and of l'Ordre Nationale du Québec and holds honorary degrees from nine universities. He also served as President of the Strategic Management Society from 1988–1991, and is an elected Fellow of the Royal Society of Canada (the first from a management faculty), the Academy of Management, and the International Academy of Management. He was named Distinguished Scholar for the year 2000 by the Academy of Management.

NITIN NOHRIA is the Richard P. Chapman Professor of Business Administration and Chairman of the Organizational Behavior Unit at the Harvard Business School. His research centers on leadership and organizational change. His latest book, *The Arc of Ambition*, coauthored with Jim Champy, examines the role of ambition in the making (and breaking) of great achievers. He is currently finishing a book, *Changing Fortunes*, that examines how large industrial corporations came to be called the "old economy" and what their future prospects might be. Professor Nohria has written or edited several other critically acclaimed books including *Breaking the Code of Change, Beyond the Hype, Building the Information Age Organization, Fast Forward,* and *The Differentiated Network,* which won the 1998 George R. Terry Book Award. Professor Nohria lectures to corporate audiences around the globe and serves on the advisory boards of several small and large firms. He has been interviewed by ABC, CNN, and NPR, and cited frequently in *Business Week, The Economist, Financial Times, Fortune,* the *New York Times,* and the *Wall Street Journal.*

JEFFREY PFEFFER is the Thomas D. Dee II Professor of Organizational Behavior in the Graduate School of Business, Stanford University, where he has taught since 1979. Dr. Pfeffer has served on the faculties at the University of Illinois, the University of California at Berkeley, and as a visiting professor at the Harvard Business School. He has taught executive seminars in twenty-six countries throughout the world and was Director of Executive Education at Stanford from 1994 to 1996. He serves on the board of directors of Actify, Audible Magic, Portola Packaging, and SonoSite, as well as on numerous editorial boards of scholarly journals. He is the author of *The Human Equation, New Directions for Organization Theory, Competitive Advantage Through People, Managing with Power, Organizations and Organization Theory, Power in Organizations,* and *Organizational Design,* and coauthor of *Hidden Value, The Knowing-Doing Gap, The External Control of Organizations,* and more than 100 articles and book chapters.

WILLIAM M. SNYDER is Founder of the Social Capital Group, a research-consulting group that helps civic organizations and businesses create community-based knowledge strategies to achieve social and economic outcomes. The organization's public-sector work includes research and consulting on civic learning networks sponsored by former Vice President Gore's office on topics such as healthy families, workforce development, and safe cities. Prior to his work with Social Capital Group, he was a core-group member of McKinsey & Company's knowledge management initiative where he helped develop organizational and technology-based approaches that were applied both within the Firm and with its clients. Dr. Snyder has twenty years of experience working with *Fortune* 500 companies—including AT&T, American Express, and Colgate-Palmolive—in large-scale change efforts that involve changing strategies as well as complex social structures and technical systems to meet shifting market requirements. He applies this organization-transformation expertise in research and consulting initiatives that help private and public sector organizations understand on a practical level what it takes to build capabilities for improved performance. He is the coauthor of the forthcoming book *Cultivating Communities of Practice: A Practical Guide to Managing Knowledge* with Etienne Wenger and Richard McDermott.

ROBERT I. SUTTON is Professor of Management Science and Engineering in the Stanford Engineering School, where he is codirector of the Center for Work, Technology, and Organization and an active researcher in the Stanford Technology Ventures Program. He is Professor of Organizational Behavior (by courtesy) at the Stanford Business School, and a Fellow at IDEO Product Development and at Reactivity. Dr. Sutton has served on the editorial boards of numerous scholarly publications, and currently serves as coeditor of *Research in Organizational Behavior*. He has published over seventy articles and chapters in scholarly and applied publications. Dr. Sutton's recent books include *The Knowing-Doing Gap: How Smart Firms Turn Knowledge Into Action*, coauthored with Jeffrey

Pfeffer, and *Weird Ideas That Work: $11^1/_2$ Counterintuitive Ways to Spark and Sustain Innovation*, which will be published in Fall 2001.

THOMAS TIERNEY is Director and former Chief Executive of Bain & Company, the international consulting firm. Mr. Tierney joined Bain & Company in 1980, was promoted to Partner after three years, and, in 1987, became Managing Director of Bain's San Francisco office, where he specialized in high growth companies and the management of service firms. Prior to his appointment at Bain, he worked for Bechtel International in North Africa as a field engineer. In 1999 Mr. Tierney launched The Bridgespan Group, an independent, non-profit affiliate of Bain & Company designed to provide Bain-quality services to foundations and non-profit organizations. He currently serves as Chairman of this endeavor. Mr. Tierney is active on a number of boards, including Hoover Institution, The National Center for Public Policy and Higher Education, Woods Hole Oceanographic Institute, Harvard Business School, Committee for Economic Development, WGBH, and New England Aquarium. He lectures at Harvard Business School and has contributed to a variety of case studies and publications, including *Harvard Business Review*. He was recently profiled in the book, *Learning from the CEO*, published by Forbes.

LUDO VAN DER HEYDEN holds the Solvay Chair in Technological Innovation at INSEAD where he teaches in the MBA, Executive, and Ph.D. programs. Prior to this appointment he was Associate Dean of Research & Development, Co-Dean, and the first holder of the Wendel/CGIP Chair in the Large Family Firm. His main areas of research focus on economic and process aspects in operations and innovation. In addition to this work, Dr. Van der Heyden is currently conducting a survey with other INSEAD colleagues on the best plants in France and Germany. His publications have appeared in several leading academic journals.

ETIENNE C. WENGER is a globally recognized thought leader in the field of communities of practice and their application to business. A pioneer of the "community of practice" research, he was the coauthor with Jean Lave of *Situated Learning*, where the term was coined. More recently, he was the author of *Communities of Practice: Learning, Meaning, and Identity*. He was featured by *Training Magazine* in their "A New Breed of Visionary" article. By helping organizations apply these ideas through consulting, workshops, and public speaking, Dr. Wenger's work is influencing the knowledge strategy of a growing number of organizations in the private and public sectors. He also teaches online courses on communities of practice and is a founding member of CPsquare, a practitioner's consortium on communities of practice.

Index